Walk Through Sprinklers

By Doraina Pyle

Copyright 2017. All rights reserved.

TABLE OF CONTENTS

WALK THROUGH SPRINKLERS 11
THANK YOU FOR THE DUCKIES 13
COUNT YOUR MANY BLESSONS 16
MY SOCK DRAWER RUNNETH OVER 17
PATIENCE, GRASSHOPPER 19
DEAL WITH THAT 20
GETTIN' JOY OUT OF THE RUT 21
I WANT THE WORLD, THE WHOLE WORLD, AND I WANT IT ON A GOLD PLATTER NOW! 23
TRYING TO FIT EN 24
CANNING HAPPINESS 25
FOREVER CHANGED 26
CHANGE AND WHINE 28
A JOURNEY THROUGH THE CENTER OF THE WILDERNESS . 30
BUT THEN THERE IS NEW GROWTH 32
LET'S MAKE A DEAL 34
JUST KEEP SWIMMING 36
JUSTICE FOR ALL 37
THE UNMISTAKABLE 39
THE UN-STEP FORWARD 40
TRY NOT TO THINK 42
STABLE GROUND 43
ROOTING OUT BITTERNESS 44
THE BLAME GAME 46
DOWN BUT NOT OUT 48
CHOOSE YE THIS DAY 49
GRIEF, BE BRIEF 51
EYES ON THE TARGET 52
OH DISTRACTION, DISTRACTION 54

A Pretty Picture	56
Restoring the Illusion	58
Love Yourself	59
Get a Grip	60
Add Vitamin C	61
To Your Health	63
To Cleanse and Protect	65
The Beauty of Kindness	66
Ouch! Rejected	68
The Overextension	70
With All Due Consideration	71
What It Means to Me	72
A Dash of Politesse	73
Speak Your Mind	75
The Word Watch	76
Pick a Little, Talk a Little	77
Thoughts on the Grapevine	78
Hold Your Tongue	80
The Heat is ~~On~~ Off	82
It's Better Unrehearsed	85
Put a Rein on It	87
Seeing What Is	88
Brick by Brick Hubris	89
The Purity Aromatic	91
Dance, Dance, Yeah	93
In Due Time	95
Fully Committed	96
Those Blasted Little Things	98
Back to Basics	99
By Their Fruits	100

Keep It Clean, Folks	101
Now You See Me	103
An Honest Day's Labor	104
Giving You the Best That I Got	106
I Can Be Bothered	108
To Lead or Not to Lead	109
Taking Thumbs Out of the Pot	111
Step Into My Shoes	113
Whoa! Slow down, buddy	114
No Other Gods	116
Evening the Scales	118
When the Time for Decision Arrives…	120
Building a Personal IRA	121
The Magic of Midnight	122
Self-Improvement 101	123
Work While You Wish	125
A Little Healthy Competition	127
Won't You Be My Neighbor?	128
Looking Past Appearances	129
Too Many Assumptions	130
Beware the Cray	132
Exclude-Me-Not	133
In the Mush Pot	134
Look at that Beauty	136
All or Nothing	137
Finding Neutral Ground	140
Bully for Him	141
Color-Coordinated	143
The Spice of Life	145
A Whole New World	147

FRIENDS, FRIENNIES, FRENEMIES?	148
BLAST THAT MANIPULATION!	150
GIVE ME LIBERTY!	151
NOM NOM NOM	153
TO EACH HIS TURN	155
HEADS AND TAILS	157
DO YOUR RESEARCH	158
THE RELIGION BEAT	159
FROM THE HORSE'S MOUTH	161
THE KNOWLEDGE APPRENTICE	162
USE YOUR SMARTS	163
YOU BETTER WAKE UP AND…	164
UNDERSTANDING GREEK AND SUCH	165
I HAVE BEEN MISTAKEN	167
MASTER AND CAPTAIN	169
ALL BY MYSELF	171
BEING YOUR OWN PERSON	173
I.D.'S THE LIMIT	175
CRAVING NICETIES	177
ROMANCING WRONG	178
LET'S TALK ABOUT IT NOW	179
A DATING DO	180
THE BLIND SPOT	182
THE HE-SHE PHENOMENON	184
THE ROOT OF ALL HEARTACHE	186
THE GREAT SWITCHAROO	188
AND LOVE, TRUE LOVE	190
SAY SOMETHING	191
MARRIAGE MATTERS	193
TEACH AND PREACH, PAPA	195

We Are Family 197
Turn Around 199
Player Wannabe 200
Thwarting Power-play 201
Be Ye One 202
The Heart of the Matter 203
Cool it with the Force 204
There Will Always Be One 205
So Hung Up 207
The Compliment Conspiracy? (Not hardly.) 209
Considering Backlash 211
Having the Conversation 213
Shhhhhh 215
Don't Shoot the Monster 216
Owning the Bad Guy Within 218
Sue Happy 220
Forgiveness and all that Stuff 222
Breaking the Seal 224
Arms folded, fingers crossed 225
Determination Decision 226
The Heartful Referee 228
Ready, Set, Fight 230
Success Unlimited 231

Walk Through Sprinklers

Let's face it: All work and no play makes Jack, Wendy, and everyone else pretty darn dull.

Yeah, sure, life is serious, and we've all got more than a few heavy matters on our plate, but it's not supposed to be furled brows and protruding lower lips all the time.

Every once in a while, we need to shout "Opa!" and smash a few plates. We've got to let our hair down and have a little fun. Throw in a little tomfoolery. Maybe an extra cookie or another half hour.

We must walk through sprinklers.

If you know me, then you know this isn't easy. I come from a long line of workaholics. We could have our own support group. It is, however, the advice I give myself quite frequently.

It came to me years ago by way of a friend. We were walking uphill – or rather, I was plowing ahead, leaving her to stare at my backside – when we walked past a house that had its sprinklers on.

I went by. She went through them.

That's when I realized sometimes I'm a little too serious.

Look, from now until forever, there will invariably be problems. Some might disappear, many may diminish, and others reoccur. Opposition is inevitable. It's a part of life.

How we handle it, though, is up to us. We can choose to laugh. We can seek joy in the toughest of moments, allowing those tidbits of delight to intersperse through our mind and change our outlook.

It's almost as if we need to let them in, else how will we survive the "REDRUM"? There's not always a fast answer or a snowcat in the woods. And even if there were, who would want that chaos?

Chaos is what makes us crazy. It's how we suffocate ourselves.

And so, I have put together this book. Basically, it is a book of principles that have simplified my life, that have increased my level of happiness. Take what you will from it.

You may find some themes repetitive – yes, repetitive – and that's okay. (I grouped them by topic.) Sometimes my inspiration came from watching the news! Same story, different cast. Every time, I couldn't help but think, "Have we still not mastered this? Really? Get back to basics, people." Then there are my experiences. Oh my, have I been schooled!

Instead of harboring anger, I write. Writing is great therapy. It makes me free, and I can deal. After I write, things are somehow okay. I can find the beatific. And wouldn't you know it? Life flows better because I can smile.

THANK YOU FOR THE DUCKIES

While I am fully aware of and believe certain truths, every now and then I have an "off day" – a day in which everything seems to conflict with what I hold sacred. The other day was one such case, where no matter how many times I listened to "Come on, Eileen," I could not shake the feeling. It was as though I had been forgotten by the Lord.

I was stressed. Recently, a decision had been rendered which left me in charge of organizing a particular event. The date was fixed, and the building scheduled. All that remained were the details: what two hundred attendees would do at the event, decorations, purchasing, volunteer coordinating, food, etc. In essence, there would be three weeks in which to get everything planned, purchased, and executed. No big deal, right? I called a meeting and four out of a potential thirty showed. Of those four committee members, only three would be in town when the event took place. Despite this, we did our best to brainstorm, and I left with some ideas.

Now, let me be clear - organization does not intimidate me. In the pre-mortal life, when gifts were being distributed, I may or may not have intercepted the ability to set matters in order for the masses. My mother thinks I should have been a wedding planner. Who knows? Perhaps I missed my calling in life. I am a master organizer; it is one of my strengths, to the point where I now assist individuals and offices with this matter. What bothers me is procrastination. I have never been, nor ever will be, one that puts off what needs to be done. Do it now; don't wait to get it done. That being said, if I had my druthers, planning for this event would have started months ago.

Because of other issues, however, it had to wait.

And so, I was stressed.

After inhaling and exhaling the air from here to China, and singing a couple of too-ra-loo-rye-ayes, I knew what I needed was a plan: an outline of the building area, a list of materials, and a course of action. I set to work on a blueprint of specifics and created thereafter a to-do list. Each day I made sure to accomplish a few items. On Tuesday, I realized I was down to the last details, which included purchasing rubber duckies. The problem was I needed a large flock of ducks, and at best, my cute bathroom friends were $3.97 for a bag of eight. I had a fifty-dollar budget. *Well*, I thought, *I will try one more store, and if they don't have a better offer, I will come up with an alternative, albeit duckfree, activity.*

By this point, I was tired. To dedicate daily the time and effort to pull off such a feat on top of life's other responsibilities is wearisome – both physically and emotionally. It was just ducks, but with compounded fatigue and heightened feelings, I was ready to quack. After all, whispers the adversary, if the Lord remembered me, He could take care of this problem, simple as it is. He is omnipotent; He can do whatever He desires. So, if He hasn't ,then…. Obviously, my mind was wandering into some wrong-thinking.

Feeling a bit defeated, I struggled to move forward. I decided I would tend to other details before heading to the store over the weekend. On Wednesday, I made my way to the supply closet, with the intent to collect needed items and assemble them together into one place. I pulled out napkins, glue, and crayons, and put them to the side. Though I had previously made a closet inventory, the minutiae of the decorations box were a bit vague. Simply put, I had only listed "Holiday décor."

Moving other boxes, I opened the lid and began rummaging. I could see what I needed was at the bottom of the bin. Keeping focus, I shifted the remaining contents elsewhere – including a stuffed, brown paper bag. *That's odd*, I thought. As I gave it a squeeze, it made a sound like a chew toy. *Clearly, this isn't relevant*, so I set it aside.

But then, I had a prompting. You know, a heavenly, instructional thought that I wouldn't have had by myself: *Look inside the bag*.

Not wanting to disregard inspiration, I picked up the sack, admittedly confused. To my surprise, as I unrolled the top, I discovered *14 yellow rubber duckies*.

At that moment, I felt my legs give out from under me. There was a rush of emotion, as once more I understood that the Lord does love me, and He is aware of every detail – however ridiculous it may be. And while we may have off-days every now and again, we can be reassured in moments like these that He cares. Stress or situation should never deter us from this truth. When things get bad, we must hold on, and do our best to keep moving ahead. Answers will come.

That night, as I knelt to pray, I had happy tears in my eyes. As I opened my mouth, I couldn't help but whisper to my sweet Father in Heaven, *Thank you for the duckies.*

COUNT YOUR MANY BLESSONS

Truth: Life is not always pretty. If anything, it's pretty *messy*, like six-cans-of-Coke-rolling-onto-the-floor-and-spewing-all-over-the-walls-the-dogs-and-your-shirt-and-pants-when-you've-got-somewhere-to-be-kind-of-messy. More often than not, it comes packaged differently than what you expected. You start with certain "I'm going to do this"-s, and while you work toward them, you circle, spiral, and zigzag everywhere on these "alternative" routes. (Who knew there were so many?)

Some days, the journey is picturesque, and on others, it is an aggravation.

In hindsight, at least you can say you learned something (or so you wish): Lessons about life, something about love, insights into your soul, if Freud was crazy or on par... Whatever it is, you have gained some sort of knowledge, which will no doubt influence your next steps, and hopefully, for the better. Now you keep a mop next to the table.

So then maybe – just maybe – taking these roads has done more than just wear out your shoes and your patience. Maybe they have been some sort of a blessing... a lesson... a blesson! (Gesundheit!)

And if you understand life is all about blessons, shouldn't you have cause to rejoice? You don't have to wait until you've reached the end of the road or arrived at greener pastures to experience joy. If you can recognize struggles serve a higher purpose, then you know that you can be happy mid-blesson!

So be sure to count them daily to experience felicity on a regular basis.

My Sock Drawer Runneth Over

Recently, my mom recalled this story from my youth:

Shortly after the family merger, the local grocer started having deals on donuts, and my stepfather thought it might be nice to treat our newly-blended group to a few of these treats. After all, what child doesn't like donuts? Each time Papa arrived home with a box, the five us would near-tackle him with excitement. Once the pastries were distributed and the bedlam subsided, there were echoing "mmmms" and "aaahs" all around.

Within six months, the situation changed. We developed preferences that transformed into uncompromising demands. Whereas we had previously loved any donut that came before us, now we could only eat the "pre-approved" or favorite. "Give me a cream cheese Danish." "No, I only want a bearclaw." As criticism replaced gratitude, we became contentious, and sadly, my stepfather was left with no choice but to discontinue the donuts.

If only we could have realized how appreciation – or the lack, thereof – affected our mindsets.

If we were to stop and count our blessings, no doubt we would have been "surprise[d] at what the Lord has done." We have been given health, sunshine, rain, shelter, indoor plumbing (Thank the heavens!), electricity, abilities, talents, senses, work, improvement, animals, friends, family, the earth, technology, freedom, and much, much more.

In fact, the blessings extend to even the littlest of things. For example, the other day, as I put away my laundry, I discovered I couldn't fit all my socks in the drawer. Thanks to my freaky foot fetish, there were too many! At first, I thought, "Now what I am going to do? Where am I supposed to put these?" Seconds later, like an epiphany (or a bastinado to the head), I was struck with, "Oh, how I am blessed! My sock drawer runneth over."

As we keep grateful, the promises are sure: Our dispositions will change for the better, and we will realize how truly rich we are.

PATIENCE, GRASSHOPPER

Imagine waking up tomorrow in an alternative reality. I.E: When the alarm sounds, you open your singleton eyes to find yourself married with six children and a set of twins on the way, set to embark on a musical tour akin to the Partridge family.

Sounds a bit crazy, doesn't it? I can't say I'd be able to handle it. Frankly, I am not ready.

Why, yes, I would love the hubby, the kids, and the painted school bus, but if they were handed to me all at once, I would need a paperbag and a breathing coach.

The same applies to other life desires; I need them piece-meal or I will asphyxiate.

For practical purposes, it is good "Everything takes time." The process gives us a chance to prepare for what is to come, a moment to learn essential life lessons, though the foot-tapping, watch-checking, "When is this ever going to happen?" part of myself might disagree.

We need not worry; our dreams will come true. Petit à petit, l'oiseau fait son nid. In other words, over time and through our efforts, we will achieve success, to include a thriving business, healthy bodies, and lasting friendships, to say the least.

Because, as Mr. Franklin says, "He that can have patience can have what he will."

Deal With That

Whether at the office or on assignment, it is not always easy working with other people. Honestly, they can be frustrating, especially if they are feckless, coming in at eleven, leaving at two, and taking a lunch in-between, later complaining that they are behind on their work.

They may not see it, and therefore, they do not change. And so, despite meticulous organization, meetings and activities never go as planned. There is just no way to anticipate outcomes.

And unless we have the means to teletransport into a life of solitude, we have to associate with these people, even though we may not want to. That is life (bum bum buuuuum).

Every day we must do our best to handle our interactions with others with some semblance of comity. There may be times when we have to walk away. We might have to reassess our communication strategies. Most likely, we will have to learn to be a little more flexible, while we lead by example. If still nothing changes, and we're at wit's end, then it is time for us to contemplate a marvelous disappearing act... and change scenes.

In whichever our approach, our manner should reflect grace. After all, these irksome individuals are our brothers and sisters. Let niceness grow, and as you persist in politeness, your dealings will transition from tolerance into love.

Gettin' Joy Out of the Rut

If you have gotten into the pattern of "Same stuff, different day," rest assured you are not alone. We are creatures of habit, which means we tend to follow a routine. Rarely do we vary from it.

Day-after-day we do this and follow it with that. Don't throw off my groove, old man.

It is not always fun; however, we know certain things must be accomplished. After all, we're supposed to feed our children more than macaroni and hot dogs every night and try to pay our bills pre-arrears.

That being said, when it comes to the point where you feel like you have fallen into this vast, ginormous rut, what do you do? Stay in the dirt? How do you re-find joy in the monotony?

Most people would suggest a new hobby – something novel to "liven up" the ennui. Hey, why not take up knitting? Go to a Taekwondo class. Have you ever considered tapdancing? Painting? Long-distance running? Mix up the mundane, why don't you?

These are fabulous ideas. If you were to stir something supplemental into the everyday, it would spice it up.

Unfortunately, this is sometimes easier said than done. As many might claim, they have jam-packed schedules that leave almost no room to breathe, let alone throw in additional activity. There simply isn't time. I've got to have at least 4.2 hours of sleep.

This is where those people must change the "little things" in their daily grind. For example, a new shampoo. A different route to work. They could have another cereal for breakfast, or look for an offbeat place to read. Maybe listen to a podcast.

Wear neon socks. Might I suggest cinnamon toothpaste? Holy cow, it's delicious.

There are always alternatives. It is just a matter of finding them. If we are willing to look, they will be there, pointing us to fresh ideas that are sure to give extra flavor to the good ol' humdrum of life.

I Want the World, the Whole World, and I Want It on a Gold Platter NOW!

Oh, dear! Has the world caught a case of Veruca Salt syndrome or what? We want those results, and we want them NOW! If we don't get them in our timetable, there will be war atop the Eggdicator.

It doesn't matter what it is – food, weight loss, money, political change – when we are ready for it to be different, we are intolerable to anything else. So, what if it has been two weeks? Who cares if it has been a day? Gimme gimme gimme.

And yet, deep, deep, deep down, subconsciously we know that everything takes time. We get how it is always a process. Seeds become trees... in time. Babies grow-up... in time. There will forever be time in matters of development and change. Heck, even Ramen needs a few minutes.

What's the world to do? Accept delayed text messages?

The answer (wait for it): Be patient.

I know that's not what you want to hear. Is it ever? Of course not! Who are we kidding? It would be nice to have our desires fulfilled instantaneously. If that guy shows up at the door with an engagement ring, I'm saying yes! It would be nothing short of miraculous.

But crazy enough, that's not how life works. And so, enjoy the scenery. Appreciate the chase. We must do our part to make the most of what is, while we work for what we want it to be.

Trying to Fit En

Oh, the joy that is life! The air, the moon, those pizza-flavored Combos! Only it is not always joyful, is it? There is an unending barrage of tests (AKA humbling life experiences) that can bog us down. And sometimes, it is just so plain taxing, we take out discouragement. Hello, Mr. Negativity. You're so cool. Shall we hang?

Lovestruck, there he stays an indefinite amount of time – because we let him.

Why do we do this to ourselves? Well, it could be genetics. Maybe we are prone to believe the worst, even if the best is also a possibility. It might have something to do with experience; nothing good has ever happened to us before…. Why should this be any different? It's been 12 years, and we're stuck in the same cycle. Wash. Rinse. Repeat. The colors have faded.

Whatever the case may be, if we have this ability to be pessimistic, then likewise, we are capable of being optimistic. The question is, are we trying to squeeze in 'en'? Namely, encouragement, energy, enlightenment, endurance, endowment, endeavor, enthusiasm… and maybe a few enchiladas? Are we willing?

They might not be as popular (save the enchiladas), but they are worth the consideration. If we worked hard enough, surely positivity would come back in fashion.

It's possible. If a naked and nailed Eric Idle can sing, "Always look on the bright side of life," surely you can too. You've made it this far; you have a 100 % survival rate. Why not get chummy with cheerful? It's enjoyable.

Canning Happiness

Wouldn't it be nice if we could can happiness the same way we do peaches? If we could seal up those merry memories and stow them away in the pantry of our thoughts, pulling them out for cheer on those cold, upsetting days?

Joy would be proud. She would appreciate the effort to hold onto those colored orbs.

And an effort it would be indeed.

As emotional, volatile beings, we are quick to bottle anger and harbor grudges. We forever remember injustices from ages past, especially if the other person seems to have "progressed" and we have not. Submarined in our souls is this struggle with faith and fear. When something happens, generally these are the first sentiments to emerge.

And yet, hope need not be fleeting, or rather, it should not.

Instead of dwelling on and associating wrongdoing with certain people, objects, and experiences, how about making it a priority to seek for something uplifting to pack and seal into our minds? Some sort of treasure that reminds us of the savory goodness we experienced?

(Note: That's not to say we become naïve, but alternatively, we learn to practice clemency.)

As we put more of these ideas into our conscience, we will build up an optimistic reserve – one so large that when other challenges come, we can pop open the jar and draw strength to pull through – with a sappy grin on our face.

Forever Changed

Whenever I smell mimosa, I remember my childhood. Next to the dining room was this beautiful mimosa tree, and with the windows open and a touch of wind, its sweet perfume would permeate our home. Sometimes I would sit under that tree and play with the little pink flowers as they fell.

I love that scent. It is my favorite tree, and every time I see one, the olfactories go into overdrive.

And isn't that just how we are? We associate an object (or a gamut of them) with a particular memory. Here's a tiny butterfly; the show we used to see; his favorite song. They remind us of loved ones and special moments.

Regrettably, some affiliations aren't always pleasant.

In these recalls, there may have been unfairness, a definite wrongdoing. Consequently, negative emotions resurface, to include dudgeon at the villainy of it all.

Two things are certain: There's no way to rewrite the past, and it does nothing to wish ill-will on anyone. It's not a victory if it is at someone else's expense. Sure, at some point we would love for others to "get it," but there's no guarantee that they will. Ever. They may stay benighted, never knowing how they crushed your heart.

With reminders everywhere, how do you get past these life-changing moments? Like the mimosa, the association is forever there.

The truth is you don't. What happened in the past made you what you are today. It led you to this point. Thus, it can never be forgotten.

What you can do, though, is get rid of the pain; the hostility that returns with the recurrence. This comes as you focus on all the good things you've got going in life. It increases as you rebuild trust – trust that one day all will be righted, and somehow everything works out as it should.

Finally, if this or that something-or-another just can't keep you from thinking about whatever-it-was that ruffles your peace of mind, make a new connection with it. Create a fresh, amazing memory to associate with that reminder. Then, when it hits the senses, it, too, will be a a positive experience.

CHANGE AND WHINE

At a previous employment, my boss used to say, "Nothing annoys me more than when a person argues, 'but this is how we've always done it.' People! Let's open our minds to new possibilities."

For most, change is a somewhat painful transition, comparable to permanent growing pains. We are creatures of habit. We drive a precise way to the post office and sit week-after-week in aisle one, pew three at church. We buy a certain brand of bread and touch our food to our chin before we eat it.

In addition, we have specific ideas of perfection, as well as visions of protocol: "If it is to be done, it should be done this way." Anything else would be a thousand marks short of impeccable. In our minds, all should adhere to this cookie-cutter standard.

When things don't go our way (and you know they won't always), we have a tendency to protest, to shout with the baritone voice of Tevye, "Tradition!"

And yet, change – even the most unwelcome of it – can be good. In fact, it can be great, a most marvelous occurrence! As one (unknown) author phrased it, "If nothing ever changed, there would be no butterflies."

Change introduces opportunity; it broadens knowledge and brings discovery. It provides those special moments where we can learn wisdom and how to make decisions. It invites us to ponder the past, enjoy the present, and contemplate the future.

Don't expect anything to stay 'as is' because frankly, it won't. Deal with those metamorphoses as best you can, aiming for some sort of happy medium.

We cannot be in charge of everything, nor should we dismiss the creativity of others. Sometimes being supportive means accepting variation.

And so, stuff your mouth with crackers, take a swig of water, and swallow. Muster some ebullience. All is going to be just fine, even if it is a little mushier than the usual.

A Journey through the Center of the Wilderness

Whether for grandma or a curse-breaking object, at some point in each of our lives, we must venture into the woods.

Yes, over the river and into the wilderness of life we are compelled to go, so as to reach our ultimate destination and outcome.

We must be tested and tried.

Sometimes, however, I feel we misunderstand the concept, for it appears many of us get stuck in the thicket of discouragement and the limbs of impossibility. No matter what we do or how we articulate the problem, nothing seems to change. In depressed tones, we conclude, "This is my life. Bring on the country music. I've got a permanent seat on the Strugglebus."

But our Father did not send us into the wild to set up camp or to befriend the R.O.U.S.s. This was not to be a lasting resting place of continual suffering (hence, the lack of cement).

Eventually, we are to emerge – and emerge victorious.

As I have reflected on my wildernesses, I have come to conclusion that to proceed I must take the following actions (which I will hereby apply to us all):

1) Stop being angry.

Like a lesson from Frozen, we need to "Let it go." No sense allowing hatred to obscure our vision, impair our abilities, and kill our compassion, as it did Roger Chillingworth. We ought to focus on what we can do to move forward. No doubt we can beat the Hitlers of the world by using our energy to do what is right.

2) Discover the lesson(s).

Turn off the TV and listen. There is a reason for everything. Throw out the "Why, woe is me?" and ask, "What am I to learn from this experience?" Most likely, the answer is "Something about me." (Well, and patience. Isn't everything about patience? Has anybody ever had a patience-free trial?)

    3)   Serve and work hard.

Cut Great Birnam Wood to advance toward Dunsinane. By doing something – even if it is only a little each day – we can move closer to where we want to be and taper the impatience that comes when things are not as we would have them now.

Trials are never easy, but we can get through them. We can work our way through the woods of life and come forth stronger, more refined, and maybe more tan. (Or, for some of us, a darker shade of pale.)

In any case, we must begin and finish the journey. We must reach our promised land.

But Then There Is New Growth

Generally, I am a huge fan of thunderstorms – that is, if I'm home. In many ways, they seem magical. There is a dominant, almost majestic, power associated with thunder and a brilliance of illumination correlated with lightning. And to be snuggled in blankets with doggies and a book to witness it all… it is comforting, even peaceful.

Occasionally, though, there are moments when I do not relish in the storm.

Such was the case the other week when rainy sheets disrupted a much-needed REM. The thunder was pompous in his declarations and his partner ostentatious with her presentations. Too much shake and flash. Throw in a blubbering wind and water pooling, and I was eyes-wide-open at 3 a.m. with no chance of return to peaceful slumber. As I lay sighing, several questions (AKA worries) came to mind:

Was the fence still intact, or had it reached its demise? Was hail forthcoming? If so, where could I move my car? Did I roll up my windows? Remember the one time I didn't? That was a nightmare. It smelled like wet socks for a week. No, they're up. Had the streets flooded? What was the damage?

Wow, I thought, welcome to the world of Negative Nancy. This can't be right. When it rains, it pours… but then there is new growth. If I look closely, I will see it – beautiful germination from what was once dry and thirsty ground (see Isaiah 44:3). Moreover, I continued, when I walk outside in a few hours, the air will be fresher, the leaves greener, and my car cleaner. While there may be some damage, if I adjust my focus, I will detect healing.

So, too, it is with the trials of life. They may appear to be disruptive, doing more harm than good. They might feel inconvenient or overwhelming or consuming. We may have more than our fair share that tend to last indefinitely.

But, these struggles are given to make us better, to sanctify our souls. They help us understand truth and strength of character. They teach us to cultivate trust and to let go of worry of what we cannot change. They purge impurity. They force new direction. They are humbling.

When we align our viewpoint to Father's, we can perceive our new growth (and its precursors) as a source of happiness.

Let's Make A Deal

Do you ever feel like you are being dealt the same hand over-and-over again? That somehow, no matter the deck or the dealer, after the cards are scrambled, shuffled, and the top card burned, you always end up with the two of clubs? Maybe in multiples, if that were possible?

The jackpot builds at table center, and for a moment you experience a tiny glimmer of hope.

"This could be mine," you whisper to yourself.

Then you remember that blasted Bill Murray curse. No need to check your hand, it rests unchanged. Maverick wins again.

Yep, it can be downright exasperating.

Sometimes we feel this is life: an unending and repetitious cycle of similar trials and other blarney, a perpetual "Oh, no, not this again!" coupled with "What!?! I've done this before." Same plot, different players. We're on a redundant (and tiresome) losing streak; we can't break this circuit.

But even in the most dismal of cases, the odds are ever in our favor because of the instruction to be gained. Quite simply, it is about "dealing with the hand you have been dealt," figuring out the purposes behind the recurrence.

For example, are there traits to acquire or virtues to develop that we didn't pick up the last round? Is it a question of trust, where we must believe we can win despite what we have been given? Perhaps the tedium could be a catalyst to prayer. Often when we can't see past what is before us, our only option is to ask the House for mercy, conversing with Him on the need to change suits and scene (not so much in negotiation as in earnest request).

Could the lesson be an issue of bravery? Some situations require courage and a possible bluff to keep the ranch. Maybe we need to up the ante, and take more risks.

Have we mastered the ability to let go? As my uncle says, "You can't hold onto everything." Sometimes, as a strategy, you must split your hand to come out ahead. At other times, it is about tossing the unnecessary.

Perhaps we need to strengthen *or break* our deck to increase our chances.

Or it may be we just need to play a different game.

In any case, if the chips are down, don't lose heart. If you can grasp the meaning despite the stale and inveterate, continuing to play come whatever is dealt, somehow all will come out + EV.

JUST KEEP SWIMMING

If you are nose-deep in the trench of despair, curled up in fetal position, trying to take cover from the bullets of life, then chances are you need assistance – at minimum, words of encouragement.

While complications may not disappear, the ability to combat them will strengthen. After all, fox holes were not meant to be places of surrender, but rather, positions in which to fight.

Life can be rough, and often events do not go as planned. For 50 years, Fraulein Maria has sung "**when** the dog bites" and "**when** the bee stings" – not *if*. Things are going to happen, and there will be times when we feel it is getting the best of us, that the doors are jammed and the Windex isn't working.

What's a person to do? Stock up on bandages and peroxide. It is time to persevere! Find new cover, and add to your infantry. Move rocks into a pile; throw out sand. Make some mud. Build a bridge. Take whatever the wind blows your way, and put it with your artillery.

In fish speak, "Just keep swimming."

Yes, follow the fish. You have come this far, which means you are strong. You have overcome much, which means you are capable.

Use whatever remaining energy you have to nab those blessings, and eventually, you will succeed! You will find that relief from the heat, weird animals, and others. You will reach an oasis, where your thirst will be quenched and you'll be able to shower.

JUSTICE FOR ALL

Forget ironic, Alanis, sometimes life just isn't fair: You face a myriad of health problems, despite your strict regimen. Your co-worker gets paid thousands more to work six hours a week, while you clock in at forty. It did rain on your wedding day, and the sun was guaranteed.

It happens.

In examining status feeds alone, sometimes it feels as though the entire world has great stuff happening, and you are bootless. Then you feel resentful. And why shouldn't you be, you reason? You're a good person. Hand over those bragging rights – things should be going on for you too!

When they're not, you want to stamp your feet and scream, "It's not fair!"

Really, though, there are only two types of fair: state and county. As the expression goes, "nothing else in life is fair."

And in case we think otherwise, no one has a problem-free life. That person's "status" reflects his or her high points.

This leaves each of us with the choice on how to handle our reaction to life's funny moments. When given those zesty lemons, what do we do? Do we moan about their shape and criticize their flavor? Do we stick out our tongues and make goofy faces? Would we rather they were mangos? Can you imagine if they were brussel sprouts?

The age-old advice has been to make lemonade, thereby turning sour into sweet. But we are not limited to liquid or culinary use. Ever heard of lemon cookies or household cleaner? Face and foot scrubs? Yep, all this and more can be done with this simple, yet pungent yellow fruit.

Sometimes it all comes down to trust, a belief that there is a Higher Power, and that He has a plan better than anything we could imagine. Indeed, the exams He gives are hard, but there are purposes – even unknown purposes – for them. It is our duty to seek them out. The sour parts we swallow can invigorate our spirits, making our senses more acute to the positive in our surroundings, helping us to be more appreciative of the sweetness of life.

And somehow, with this perspective, we can deal with the understood inequalities in love and war.

The Unmistakable

To err is human, but it is certainly not Divine. God is not the author of mistakes. He created us, His children, in His image, and He created us perfectly. With an individualized plan, every child has been given specific flaws or challenges to develop His attributes while striving to work with or overcome them.

To be honest, some of these temptations are harder than others. Goodness knows there are those who suffer and struggle for years with issues far greater than we could ever imagine. It can be a constant battle to find and maintain identity or even just figure things out. (For all, we express our sympathy and unconditional love. Keep the flame of hope burning.)

In these instances, more spiritual reinforcement than normal is needed. One does not go to battle armed with a loin cloth. There must be preparation – some sort of strategy –to conquer: a helmet, a shield, Matthew McConaughey on the bongos. Each day requires maximum effort to ensure the supernal protection necessary to move forward.

There may be situations we don't enjoy. Take comfort. We have knee-mail and the good news of the Gospel. Moreover, we can learn to focus on what we like and what we can change without hampering our Divine natures.

Like the TV show, Father knows best. He always has, and He always will – make no mistake.

The Un-Step Forward

At one point or another, most of us have devised some sort of life plan. Tell me if this sounds familiar:

- "By the time I am 23, I will be married with two children."
- "I will finish my Doctorate before I reach 30."
- "In another five years, I will own a house and have a career. In ten I will…"

You set your goals, make an outline of each step of the process, commence working toward them, and BAM!

The unexpected happens, and everything changes.

- There is an accident, and now you are primary caretaker of a family member.
- The company is sold to a competitor, and you lose your job.
- You enter graduate school sure of what you want to do and exit dumbfounded.
- You quit a $95,000 job to sell ice cream in the Caribbean because you feel disenchanted.
- For love, you follow a guy to Harvard, only to become a lawyer and fall for Emmett.
- The love of your life puts you out of business with the assurance it's "nothing personal."

Your whole world has been rocked!

Suddenly, you are thrown off course, feeling somewhat and/or completely lost. Can anything else go wrong? "This wasn't part of the program!" you yell toward heaven.

But maybe it was.

Maybe this supposed step backward is exactly what you needed to propel you forward. You had to quit that job, move to another city, or give up on that relationship. Sure, it detours from the desiderata, but the miracle of the un-step is somehow you end up happier than you could have imagined. You gain critical development.

And this – well, this is progression. With bravery into the unknown, so long as you are getting up each day and trying, then you are forging ahead. Just because it varies from your initial conception does not mean you have failed, nor are you stagnant.

Simply put, the Lord reviewed your outline and decided to tweak it a bit. Okay, He decided to tweak it a lot. You're the only piece that stayed the same. He thought you could use more steel in your backbone.

Now it is time to maintain confidence. As you advance as planned – and unplanned – into the future, let Him steer and chase away those night tigers.

Try Not to Think

Does anyone else have these moments where you think "what might have been/if only" or is it just me? For example, what if I had gone into the Peace Corps? What if I had said something? If only I would have stayed or picked that one instead. What if, what if, if only….? If I could do it all over, I would... fill-in-the-blank.

Welcome to the world of imagination.

For the most part, these thoughts stay at bay because I am happy with my life. Every now and again, though, they creep into my head like a scene out of Sliding Doors, and I can't help wondering how differently my life would have been if I had made this choice instead of this other one. If this one moment had gone otherwise, would I have been any happier or would I have become more miserable? Would it have turned out the same way no matter what I had chosen?

Speculate all I want, there's really no way to say. Either is possible. There could have been other outcomes. Honestly, I'll never know; hindsight is a limited 20/20.

Hence the reason it is so important to appreciate the present for what it is and to choose wisely from what is placed before you. You don't want to spend any time in regret. You want to look toward the future without a sense of dread.

Life is meant to be lived and loved for what it is! If you need to look back, do it quickly, so you can return and make the most of today.

STABLE GROUND

Oh, rejection, rejection! Sighs. It is everywhere.

- Want a cookie? Too bad! You can't have it.
- What, you're not interested? I thought we were on the same page.
- Please sir, if I could only have a minute of your time... Please don't slam that door in my face!

Talk about rough. Who needs such slog?

And yet, like it or not, dismissal is always going to be there in some form or fashion. People make choices, which means we may not be accepted, no matter how much we would like to be.

Ain't that a real kick in the teeth? Might as well invest in braces.

It's a free world, so outside of illegal, you can't change what others will do.

You can only change your reaction to it.

Of course, irrationality is an option. There's nothing like throwing a super-size temper-tantrum. Why not chunk that friendship, that job, that belief system right out the window? Feed the immaturity beast; send everything back with an all-caps "RETURN TO SENDER." If it's not your way, it's no way! Who's with me? Anyone? Bueller?

Then again, there's the alternative of moving on, taking brush-off as a blessing in disguise; a chance to find new opportunities. After all, no matter what someone "has done," there is no justification for cruelty. Find freedom in forgiveness. Learn how to handle your feelings; to not take things personally. There is peace in emotional stability.

So, too, is there also stable ground.

Rooting out bitterness

It is unfortunate, but sometimes things don't work out – at least not the way we wanted them to. Despite his behavior, that person did get his way, we were overlooked, and those people remain happily married. If we were honest with ourselves, maybe we could recognize we weren't the superior choice. Maybe we were, but they decided to go with something else. We could have deserved whatever it was. Maybe we didn't.

Justice may never be served in this lifetime.

It's maddening. Believe me, I get it. The Gods have turned on more than one occasion.

So how do we work through these issues? How do we overcome? Imagine such-and-such is unhappy? (Why give them any thought at all?) Picture the company downfall? Brainstorm every feasible victory under "what might have been?" Perhaps tell everyone we meet how we were "cheated" to win their sympathy. Certainly, it would have been better if "it was you."

Or, as an alternative to the downward spiral, we could do what we can to move beyond it.

It's hard, for sure, but not impossible.

It begins with uprooting those negative thoughts and throwing them away. Hate blinds and keeps us from progression. It does no good. Curses and spells are but temporary fixes.

Next, recognize you are upset because it didn't come together like you wished. An old Tongan proverb states, "There is no pain so great as a hope unfulfilled." You expected a specific outcome – had your heart set and your toes crossed– and then.... then you were trampled. You were going for this and got **that** instead.

Doubtless it was wrong, but is *that* really so bad? Right now it is, but later on will it be?

If we could eradicate our tunnel vision, we would see other possibilities in our peripheral: another prospect in the background; an opportunity to travel; this potential job. We could date this other person, who is more amazing. Now we have more time to spend with our families.

With newfound humility, we can see what was once imperceptible.

We cannot change the past; we cannot undo what has been done. We can, on the other hand, determine our response (at least the secondary one).

If, like a plant, we stay rooted in bitterness, we will go nowhere. By contrast, when we push past disappointment, we can grow anywhere.

THE BLAME GAME

Someone once shared this with me: In the beginning, God created Adam and Eve, and when they transgressed, Adam blamed Eve, and Eve the serpent. And oh, that poor serpent! He didn't have a leg to stand on.

It was the ultimate case of passing the buck.

And thus, it has moved from generation to generation. The fault is yours, not mine. (See how I did that? What a cinch!)

It is almost as if we are programmed to blame others for our unpleasant situations, rather than take responsibility for ourselves. Some even go so far as to find wrongdoing with entire entities or organizations, like universities or churches, to the point where they transfer or leave them altogether.

This is where Truman would step in and say, "Stop it. Stop it right now."

We all fall on hard times. Things often don't go according to plan. Sometimes that is just the way it is, and we deal with it the best we can. In some cases, the outcome was self-induced. That is to say, our choice led to that result; it was this reaction that brought that consequence. Simply put, we are never absolved from our part in the matter. (Let it serve as a cautionary tale.)

It's time to own it.

It is time to make ourselves accountable.

Instead of pointing the finger at him, her, and those guys over in the corner, shift it back to ourselves. Where did we go wrong? What can we do to resolve the problem? How can we fix it?

Anyone can rise out of a rut. It takes hard work, but it can be done. It saves time when we can pinpoint and accept our share in the situation, for then we know where to focus.

Re-write your future by owning the present today.

Down but Not Out

Oh man, that did not turn out how I wanted! Boo. Boo. Boo, boo, boo.

Weeping, wailing, and seventeen hisses behind closed doors.

Talk about disheartening! In this world, there is a world of injustice. Not everything goes as it should. The wicked repeatedly seem to prevail, and quite frankly, it's disgusting. Wrong wins time and again, even though we fought for right. It's an everyday battle, with a lot of "It shouldn't have happened that way." If you're lucky, a few things might sway how you want them.

How we handle disappointment reflects our wisdom and maturity.

It would be simple to return to those hair-pulling, "meanie" days of yore; however, gone are the years, so time to forgo fit-throwing, non-stop crying in the street for a week. We are old enough to know better. We can be more private and tasteful in our expression.

There is nothing wrong with mourning. It is fair to grieve.

Take the necessary time... and then be done with it.

Life is not over because something went contrary to expectation. Maybe reality isn't good now, but that does not mean it is going to last forever. If there is any constant in life, it is "Life changes."

So, take heart! Hang in there! Tomorrow is another day, and maybe it will be better. If not, move forward as best you can, keeping bummer at bay.

Choose Ye This Day

In light of recent events, I can't help but talk about accidents and tragedy. Sometimes bad things happen, and in many cases, they happen to the best people. No matter the situation, they never make much sense, because with human logic we think, "If you are a good person, good things will happen" or "If you are righteous, no harm will come to you."

And yet, it doesn't always work that way. Why is that? Why do these things happen? It seems counterintuitive.

Please allow me to attempt at explanation.

It is never the Lord's will that someone be robbed, hurt, or murdered. God gave express charge of His behavioral expectations when He revealed the Ten Commandments to Moses. "Thou shalt not steal," "Thou shalt not kill," and "Thou shalt not bear false witness" were included among this set (see Exodus 20). Additionally, when He sent His Son, Jesus Christ, He provided a higher law for us to "Love one another."

It is, however, the Lord's will that we all have agency, or the freedom to choose, how we wish to live our lives. And while you and I may opt for kindness and integrity, not all will do the same – unfortunately. Just as there are those who have decided to love, there are others who are determined to hate. And as equally as God will let us have our agency, He will let them have their pick as well. Rest assured, at the last day all of our actions – be they good or bad – will be judged and remunerated accordingly.

While it is not always ideal – sometimes frustrating, even incredibly heartbreaking – it happens. It is another constant of life that these bad things will happen. They will happen, though, along with the good.

We need not get angry with God, for again, He has established His standards. From these we know He wants only the best of and for His children. He has set the precedent for how He wants us to interact with one another. No doubt He is saddened when we misuse our freedom of choice and behave improperly. He is not okay with 'screwing someone over,' no matter how much someone wanted something.

By the same token, we know He will support us when we are victims of said actions. Not only will He bless us with peace, helping us to overcome what would otherwise be insurmountable grief, He will give us the eyes to see the greater picture, as well as the potential positive outcomes.

It is an imperfect world, replete with imperfect people. Things are bound to happen.

Despite it all, we can control how we act and react in these situations. We can choose to stand with the Lord and help others to do the same, thereby making it a better place.

GRIEF, BE BRIEF

As the saying goes, "Nothing is certain but death and taxes."

We all know and understand this, at least to a certain degree, and still they aren't any easier. (Has anyone ever requested an audit? Hands up, who's invited the Grim Reaper to come and sit a spell?)

Taxes take their toll, and death wrenches our heartstrings, especially when it is unexpected or unexplained.

It is natural to mourn for the losses we suffer. Within our hearts, we have this void, knowing we will never laugh and swap stories with our beloved in this life again. Because of the profundity of our love and the joy of our association, it is painful to think we will have to wait to make new memories.

And so, we take as much time as we need to cope with the death. There is no set pace or limit in which to say, "See you later." We hope grief is brief, but if not, we pray that it is bearable.

At some point, we want these feelings to pass, so we can move beyond bereavement to fixating on when the person was alive. We want to remember those times we ziplined to the barn and ate all the bread. We pay tribute to that life, those sparkling blue eyes. (Maybe with an actual book of stories and pictures.)

As we celebrate the goodness, those joyful "June roses" will replace the painful sentiments of December we feel today.

For these reasons, we take heart. We find our peace. This life is but a moment, and one day, we will see all our loved ones again.

Eyes on the Target

Although it has been said before, there is no harm in saying it again: There is a lot out there competing for our attention. Combine that with thingamabobs and other whatchamacallits, and who can sit still? It is almost as if we have become a generation of ADHD, must-have-stimulation-at-every-turn-or-else-we-will-die-a-slow-and-lethargic-death kind of people.

Please don't misunderstand: Technology is a blessing, providing access to unfathomable amounts of information. Social media helps us maintain old connections, as well as establish new ones.

The problem is that the constant need to use these outlets will turn into an addiction if we are not careful. Suddenly, we are those people we see at the restaurant sitting across from each other more engaged with our phones than with each other. We have become so caught up in the hailstorm of political and social issues that we have discarded thoughts of our well-being and those of others. The birthmark is now the focal point, not the overall beauty, says Hawthorne.

How do we return to the center of that which is most important?

The answers depend on you and what you want out of life. Who would you like to be? What would you like to accomplish? If you wish to check status updates by the second, that is your prerogative.

If you desire something more, then there needs to be a change. Turn off those notifications. Issue guidelines to yourself, such as time limits in front of the screen or with an organization. Set the phone aside when there is company. Leave it in the other room or put it in the glove box! Create an incentive program with the type of rewards that will motivate you to take charge of your life and accomplish that to-do list. Schedule meditation. Cultivate relationships outside of cyberspace. Pick up a book; go out in nature. Buy a hammock.

The list is endless, and the outcome certain (even logical): When you move away from distractions, you find peace. And in that uninterrupted stillness, you can focus on what really matters.

OH DISTRACTION, DISTRACTION

As a church missionary, it was my opportunity to lead groups around one of our temples. On one such occasion, I had a youth group, and as we rounded the corner to the entrance, we stopped to have a discussion.

Mid-spiritual discourse, two leaders at the back of the group started giggling.

A bit confused, I glanced at them for clarification.

"Oh, sister! Look!" one of them gushed, pointing behind me.

My eyes followed the path of her finger point. As my focus narrowed, I identified the cause of the 8th-grade reenactment. There, by the temple doors stood the interrupter of flow, Mr. Puppy Love himself, Mr. Donny Osmond.

Now, don't get me wrong, I like Donny Osmond. He is a talented man, and I was delighted when he won Dancing with the Stars. But if David Ives is right – that is to say, if it is "All in the Timing" – then at this moment Donny's was a quarter past ill.

Doing my best to stifle the version of "Go Away Little Girl" playing inside my head, I turned to the ladies and pulled my chin back into place.

"Oh, but sister, wouldn't you?"

Unsure as to what to say, I simply shook my head and tried to recover what was left of the moment. It felt, however, that the moment was lost.

So it is with us sometimes. We make these great efforts to put ourselves in the right place at the right time, only to allow distractions to take us elsewhere. How often do we inquire about football scores? How frequently do we rationalize tardiness or irreverent behavior? Is gum really a necessity? Can we not take care of business before or after an activity? When did answering calls in the middle of class become okay? There is a time and place for everything, and we know what those are. We just want what we want when we want it.

Somehow, we have permitted these little amusements and preoccupations to creep into our thoughts... and therefore, into our actions. Not only should our doors face the right direction (see Mosiah 2:6), but our hearts and minds need to as well. It takes great discipline. As we do our best to stay focused, we will uncover greater meaning in our moments.

A Pretty Picture

Movies can be deceptive, at least most of the ones I see. They transport you into a world where problems are surmountable, questions are answered, and there are never loose ends. Everything finishes with one nice, pretty, big red bow... and a happy reconciliation with the man of your dreams.

That's probably why I like them so much. They're quite the change from everyday life.

From this day to the next, things will happen for which there are no reason. By way of illustration: The person you love picks someone else. You are unable to get pregnant. Your friend is involved in an accident. You don't get hired for your dream job, even with the education and experience. There is disease, disaster, family issues, financial hang-ups, and so forth. It can be nonstop brouhaha.

You can only adapt "the plan" so much before it gets tossed out the window. There are too many variables in which you have no control.

The struggle is real.

The trick is to not let those pitfalls get you down and to persevere, no matter how strenuous. Sometimes when we get to those "pivotal" moments – the ones that throw our entire world into a tailspin – it is all we can do to hang on. We clutch to whatever safeties we have so we don't go down with it. But it hurts like no other. The pain is undeniable, and it can last for years.

Then come the emotions: anger, hurt, depression. It is a serious battle to not allow them to overtake our determination and peace.

And when there is no foreseeable or satisfying resolution, it can be backbreaking to hold on to what you once knew to be true.

Adversity thinks we are faint-hearted. Its aim is to have us forsake any semblance of goodness; to become coarse. It wants to shake and smash our confidence. Sometimes it does a darn good job. Don't let it ruin your life. If anything, allow it to change you for the better.

If we can endure, staying strong to our principles come what may, then no matter what happens, we will have our happy ending. It may not be anything like we pictured... in fact, it'll probably be a startling (yet superior) contrast to what we imagined, with or without all those little neat ends.

But it will be.

It will be a pretty picture.

Restoring the Illusion

Sometimes horrible things happen, like earthquakes, murder, or the cancellation of Firefly. These moments are particularly painful, and generally, there is no satisfactory explanation for them. In instances where right has been compromised, there is now a disillusion with life, and in some cases, a profound level of hopelessness.

In the tug of war of emotions, villainy can bruise every millimeter of our hearts, inevitably causing us to fall with little to no hope of recovery. Now, rather than risk ourselves to new adventure or potential joy, we would prefer cocooning on the couch on a gloomy afternoon with a copy of *The Bell Jar*. Supposedly, it would be better.

But just as we wouldn't stop mid-labor or prior to cookie completion, we don't quit the race of life. The Lord wants finishers. He wants us all to win, even if it means we arrive via stretcher. To that end, we must search for that last ounce of desire to pick up whatever pieces of heart we can. Then, we give those pieces to He-who-is-Whole, and allow Him to re-align the parts and fill in the cracks, thus restoring the illusion.

Love Yourself

When you stop and think about it, we sure do a lot to our bodies these days. We are determined to enhance, pad, tuck, probe, and surgically alter until we near some weird, life-size replica of either Ken or Barbie – or both.

There are heels to compensate for shortness, girdles to rein in bellies, and make-up to coat faces. We like to dye and perm, straighten and crimp. (Long live the 80s!) We tat; we pierce; we bleach. We starve, a lot of times going beyond basic beauty maintenance into the realm of unhealthy. In many cases, we have convinced ourselves that there is no happiness until we have morphed into this ideal of our imagination.

Why do we subject ourselves to such torture? Because someone made a comment back in seventh grade that stuck? Because we were teased? We couldn't shake certain thoughts or temptations? We feel alone?

Who sets these standards? What led to this obsessive dissatisfaction?

Of course, we want to feel and look our best, but there is a fine line between that and self-induced psychological, physical, and financial torment. If we could channel our efforts into practicing acceptance, from how we were born to who we have grown up to be, we would discover bred-in-the-bone happiness. If we could appreciate our gender, the gaps in our teeth, and those sometimes uncomely "beauty marks" – these key parts of our identity – then no doubt we would understand how to love ourselves.

GET A GRIP

One of my friends likes to say, "Once we find our self-worth, we handle life better." She must be a descendent of Confucius.

Think about it. When we understand our value, we feel complete. There is no void to fill, no space to recover, no need to compensate. We realize that we have importance. We have an identity.

So, throw away the stress eating and some of that chocolate! (Gasp! Sacrilege.) With self-esteem, we don't need any additional sources to make us happy.

We can move forward with confidence, having this assurance of certain truths:

1) Our Heavenly Father loves us. Come what may (dismal days and all), He is on our side, without question. Look closely, and you will notice His tender hand in your life. He wants each child to succeed.
2) With Him, we are and have a family. Despite the paranormal things that happen, we need not feel alone. We can draw daily strength from our Divine heritage.
3) He has a specific plan for everyone. Sometimes we may be unaware of what that entails. We may question, "Hey, what's that plan again? Seriously, I don't know anymore." We feel left in a world of confusion. This is where we must trust God has a purpose and that these obstacles will dare us to become better.

In short: Make an appraisal, and learn your inestimable worth. Then shall you get a steady hold of your life.

Add Vitamin C

When life feels stationary, people tend to catch cases of the snoughfles:

Am I good enough? Smart enough? Rich, cool, or pretty enough? Am I skinny or strong enough? Talented enough? Spiritual or funny enough? "Etc, etc, etc" – Yul Brynner.

Notice a pattern?

Yeah, that's enough. Let's end it right here. It is time to build a better immune system and eradicate this illness from your life. Help your body and mind feel better with a self-imposed prescription.

Start with two tablets of encouragement every time needed. That is to say, repeat the words of Aibileen Clark to yourself wherever you are: "You is kind. You is smart. You is important." My grandpa used to greet his reflection with a boisterous "Good morning, Tiger" and subsequent pep talk. Comprehend you are enough. In fact, you are more than enough, and you have something unique to offer. Who cares if it differs from the Jones'? That's how it is supposed to be. (What a Sad Sad Sad Sad World it would be without peppermint ice cream!)

Next, gargle with protection. Now that you understand your value, safeguard it. This may require a change in habits. For example, if the constant scrutiny of Hollywood's finest leads you to question your self-image, switch to National Geographic. It is well-worth the effort to preserve your individual merit.

Finally, "for all day strong, all day long" relief, learn the difference between self-improvement and overkill. Yes, we want to develop as individuals; however, even Monk would agree, the quest for perfection is not meant to be destructive. Do your best, and contentment will follow.

Take these steps to remedy health. Side effects include satisfaction, happiness, fulfillment, and joy.

To Your Health

Every day in today's health-obsessed world, we hear variations of the following: This is full of amino acids. Try this concoction; it will help you to lose weight fast. Do this one exercise to boost metabolism. Watch out for these foods. Don't forget your greens. Eat almonds. Add blueberries. Remember your Gingko and Vitamin D. Studies show this really works. Nine out of ten doctors recommend this unpronounceable pharmaceutical that has like a billion side-effects.

The list goes on and on... Yep, there is a lot out there.

And for what purpose does it serve? Amidst the body conscious, its aim is to fit everyone into a size two for a fabulous look come summer – as if that's the only way one could be blithe. At other times, we are trying to impress the guy next door, or we think "Let's try this" because it received the First Lady's endorsement.

This is where we miss the mark. While yes, those reasons can be motivational, there are other noteworthy arguments behind adhering to a healthy regimen.

First, it is important to feel good about yourself. Forget what the world says, and set your own terms. You need to be okay with you. Remember no one has a perfect body, not even those A-list supermodels. Only in a world of airbrushing does that "standard" exist. Keep that in mind as you examine the areas you wish you could change, and do what you need to do within reason. Remember your health affects your mental and emotional states.

Second, your family and friends love you, and most likely they want you to stick around for a while. They want you in attendance for significant and what-may-feel-like-inconsequential events, such as waking up, phone calls, weddings, suppertime, baby births, first steps, smiles, board game battles, park outings, yard work, graduations, and so forth. You are an integral part of the group, which means your presence is valuable and your influence far-reaching.

Third, you have something to contribute to this world, and you need time to accomplish it. This is much easier to do when you are healthy and relatively pain-free.

No doubt as we switch these reasons to the forefront, our motivation to stay 'hale and hearty' will move there as well.

To Cleanse and Protect

Life is far too short to get tangled up in the brackish mean-spiritedness that surrounds you. We all have situations – complications aplenty – but there is no sense stirring drama in with more drama, drama, drama.

There will always be those willing to throw you every which way, be it over or under the many wheels of the semi. In a callous and ruthless attempt to get ahead, these people may divulge your secrets or even toy with your emotions. They might calumniate you and your family to get what they want. Chances are you will get dumped, replaced, or swept into the far corner beneath the Persian.

This does not mean you cut these people completely out of your life (although in some instances you do – it's your call), but you do need to safeguard yourself.

Unless your Regina George, no one walks in front of a moving bus, at least not voluntarily. You need not subject yourself to garbage. Don't ask for the arsenic. It is not worth the cost of your sanity, the damage to your well-being, or the erosion of your spirit.

Despite contrary belief, we can still be kind to others without having them trample all over us. We can protect our hearts from erratic behavior with the breastplate of Zeus, while keeping the Welcome mat on the doorstep.

The Beauty of Kindness

My father likes to tell me stories, and one of his favorites (and mine) comes from the life of Mr. Hank Greenberg, a legendary baseball player. In a time where anti-Semitism was high, Mr. Greenberg suffered much for being Jewish, especially when he refused to play on Yom Kippur during the pennant. Rather than respond with hatred, Hammerin' Hank continued on with dignity.

Later, when he witnessed another player facing social derision, Hank did something remarkable: he showed overt kindness to the so-called "outcast" by helping him up during a game after a field collision. Because of his good will, manifested through a simple gesture, Mr. Greenberg led the rest of the world in accepting and respecting Mr. Jackie Robinson as a legitimate baseball player. The rest, as you know, is history.

To me, this story paints a picture of the nature of kindness: performing genuine acts of love without hesitation for another person. It is beautiful. It is enduring. These small deeds are the greatest treasures we keep, even after we have entered the realm of dementia. Never will I forget the friend who shouted hello from a distance on one of my worst days, the sweet note from one of my students when my car was hit, or the flowers someone left on my doorstep after my grandma passed. My heart was sincerely touched by such goodness.

The challenge comes in returning kindness. Generally, it is easy to match smile-for-smile and grace-for-grace, but what do we do with mean people? The ones who are determined to hate us because we are still breathing? Those who spread lies without compunction, although they were clearly in the wrong? How can we possibly emit goodness toward those people, when secretly we would rather run them over with our car?

In my experience, it takes restraint... and an extreme amount of prayer (see Matthew 5:44). Somehow, as we plead for their good health and happy endings, we are able to let go of negativity. Thoughts transfer into actions, and overtime it becomes natural to show genuine warmth to the least likely and/or deserving of individuals. We are not bound by hatred. Truly, we are free. At that point, we find kindness is manifest, and once again, it is beautiful.

Ouch! Rejected.

Here is an interesting experience:

Recently, a group went for an outing in the local area. As they arrived on scene, they went and stood in line, as per protocol. During the wait for entry, they noticed a few members of their pack ahead and beckoned for them to fall back to combine with their numbers. They did so, allowing other patrons to move in front of them. Those who failed to arrive on time went ahead and joined in with the others, since entry was paid as a group, not as individuals.

All seemed to be okay, until a woman behind them got upset.

Sensing her frustration, those at the back of the party apologized and explained the situation to her.
Instead of accepting their whys and wherefores, the woman continued to rant, rallying those behind her to engage in hateful banter toward the members of the group. She felt the entire company should move to the end of the line, even though many had arrived before her.

For an hour, the group kept quiet and stayed calm, enduring the harangue, and upon admittance, they paid her group's admission – or at least they tried to.

The woman would have none of it! Determined to stay belligerent, the woman re-paid the entry fee, while continuing to make churlish remarks. Once inside, she spent the entire evening scowling at the other party.

That night, this woman rejected all kindnesses. She made a deliberate choice not to forgive.

How pathetic her life must be! How sad for her children, for whom she sets an example!

Unfortunately, throughout our lives, we will come across such people – those who prefer hate over love. Blackguards. We might mess up and inadvertently offend them. They may get upset for no other reason than our very presence.

If we are fortunate, the other person will accept our apology and redress.

There will be some, however, like this lady, who don't.

Notwithstanding, we must never stop being nice. Love is the only way to combat hate.

Furthermore, when we have made every effort to show remorse and make reparation, then we have done all that we can do. Therefore, we are released from further responsibility. We should forgive ourselves and move on. While human instinct aches for everyone to like and accept its offerings, if the other individual is unwilling, then it is time to walk away, no matter how difficult that may be. Remember, relationships are a shared responsibility.

Thus, the other party is accountable for the remaining resolution. After that person has eradicated the anguish that corrodes her soul, she will reach out. Most likely, it will take time, especially if she struggles with overlooking inconsequentialities, like the woman in the story.

It is not our place to impose a deadline, but alternatively, to keep our hands extended.

THE OVEREXTENSION

Everyday a janitor at a nearby facility mops all the hallway floors of the building. When he has finished, he places the required "Caution, Wet Floor" signs where they are needed to avert others to be careful.

And every day, at that same facility, an elderly gentleman goes behind the janitor to collect all the caution signs before the floors have dried. Thinking he is being helpful, he stacks and organizes them into a pile for the next use.

Whereas the elderly man's intentions are greatly appreciated, his actions are premature.

Sometimes we, too, are quick to jump the gun in offering our services. Without asking, we decide on what we feel would be best for a situation. In haste, we assume that naturally, "It must be the right thing," since everyone likes free help, right? Doesn't everyone love casserole and funeral potatoes?

If our vision is at the forefront, instead of behind our eardrums, then we might well be blinding ourselves to what is truly desired. In fact, we may be annoying a person more than assisting him.

The keystone to service is listening. What is this person asking? What does he mean? Does he want me to step in, or do I need to back away?

Although the blessings of service are far-reaching, the full extension comes as we cater to another person's actual needs, not to our own.

We may want to do everything under the sun, but first, we must wait until the floors have dried.

With All Due Consideration

With all the craziness happening in the world, sometimes I find myself asking, "When did this become okay?" I must have missed the memo. If there was smoke signal, I sure didn't see it. Have we determined it's okay to blacklist whomever for whatever, interrupt acceptance speeches (Oh, Kanye!), and take bathroom selfies?

It is almost as if we have decided, "If I want it, then it's alright. No big deal."

And yet, we know this absolute: Small acts lead to great consequences, be they good or bad.

If we wish to change the world for the better, then we must start with personal behavior.

Each of us are privy to an individualized Jiminy Cricket, who works to refine our behavior. As we apprentice his tutelage, somehow, we learn to master common courtesy and practice self-control. We rise above the cattiness "which doth so easily beset us" (Hebrews 12:1). We come to understand the intrinsic value of every person and fittingly undertake to treat one another with the utmost respect.

Then, when assessed with "Have I done any good in the world today?" most assuredly, we can respond "Yes."

What It Means to Me

R-E-S-P-E_ _

Oftentimes, it feels as though we live in a world that's missing a few Cs, Ts, Ps and Qs. There is an overabundance of callow dispositions, where many spew forth viewpoints without the least consideration for another's feelings. Some people just "can't be bothered" with anything beyond nose point.

Quite frankly, this type of attitude is disrespectful, and at its core is selfishness.

If Rodney were still alive, no doubt he would weigh in on the matter with a few humorous lessons: *I tell ya' I get no respect*.

In all seriousness, though, respect comes down to this key principle:

If you want respect, extend it to others.

In other words, live that Golden Rule. Speak well to and about one another. You can't expect someone to let you into his inner circle if he knows you've been gossiping about him.

Practice those sirs and ma'ams. No one ever hurt his jaw being polite. Consider elder and child alike as a son or daughter of God with a divine purpose. Hold all in esteem. Einstein says he spoke to everyone in the same way, whether it was "the garbage man or the president of the university."

If you want respect "when you get home," to the workplace, or wherever, keep sockin' it to this. TCB. Drop the mic.

A Dash of Politesse

This morning I had a situation. While at the park with my beloved, we passed a group of ladies walking with an unleashed dog. Naturally, the little ones were curious about each other. Mine manifested his interest through barking; theirs with approached running. We both had to use restraint to keep them separate, since it did not look like the interchange was going to pan out nicely. It happens. The second time we crossed paths, however, I heard one of the women make a snide comment purposely within earshot about my dog.

Of course, I was upset. Talk about uncalled for – not to mention, completely unnecessary. That was ridiculous. She might as well have made a "yo mama" joke and stolen my savings. It was the same effect.

Indeed, there may be times when things don't work out. We may not get along; we might annoy one another. With so many variables, our calculations can be wrong. Life is never a perfect flow of happy incidents.

That does not mean we become insulting. There is no need to be coarse. No matter the situation, we can still throw in a dash of politesse.

As Mother Teresa said (in one of my favorite quotations), "If you judge people, you have no room to love them."

Despite what transpires, it is possible to show a smidgen more consideration toward each other. We are intelligent creatures capable of self-discipline. We can choose when to speak, when to keep silent, and when to let that guy merge. We know how to communicate; how to call when we're running late; how to cancel when we feel sick; how to throw bad judgment out the window. We have eyes to notice needs and arms to open doors. We can let our feet guide us to greater service opportunities.

With a pinch here and a dollop there, we improve our flavor of civility, making for finer walks and more desirable interactions.

Speak Your Mind

Very distinctly do I remember the man who said to me, "Now that I am engaged, I can tell you – you have a pretty smile."

Puzzled at his delay, I asked him forthright, "Why did you have to wait?"

He responded, "Because I didn't want to give you the wrong impression."

Through pursed lips, I reassured him he could have shared this with me; I would not have misinterpreted his intention. In fact, had he expressed himself, it would have been a blessing, given at that point in life, I was seriously struggling.

To be crystal: It is always okay to compliment someone. We need never hold back genuine expressions of warmth.

When we hesitate, we miss out on opportunities to uplift one another. Life is challenging, to say the least, and we are all tested every day. Why should silly – often unfounded – fears keep us from sharing niceties? Who wouldn't want to feel better about life and its possibilities? We need those warm fuzzies.

Frankly, there is nothing wrong with helping others improve their self-worth – at least, there shouldn't be.

So, please, speak your mind! Shower the people around you with uplifting words.

The Word Watch

Without question, the freedom of speech is an enormous blessing! The ability to state our thoughts does much to fulfill the primary aims of the Constitution "to form a more perfect Union" and "promote the general Welfare."

Yet frequently, sandwiched between our smiles, is a chewed mouthful of sarcasm, profanity, and a whole lot of ugly. Is life really that upsetting? Must we be so casual with our cynicism? Or perhaps, like middle schoolers, this negativity is now second-nature, and we need censorship every other word?

Are we slaves to our swearing, no longer at liberty to choose wholesome communication?

Lest we forget, language is a representation of our beliefs, upbringing, and education. It reflects our level of maturity, as well as our leadership ability, and determines whether we are trustworthy.

As a society, we have come a long way since *Gone with the Wind*. Whereas once we chose carefully our words, the tendency today is to speak before we think, like some Wolf of Wall Street, to anyone we come across. We okay it with our children.

Maybe it is time to do a self-check, even analyze the impact of our social circles and media choices.

With over one million words in the English language, there is no reason why we cannot set aside the brickbat and use proper language on a regular basis, utilizing our words to uplift others and to endorse good. We have the brains. Do we have the willpower?

Pick a Little, Talk a Little

Communication is what makes us human. Much like Madonna, we want to express ourselves. (Some of us non-stop.) If, however, you have ever been the victim of gossip or have witnessed the horrible aftermath of your words, then you understand the importance of kindness. You know to think twice before sharing all that is on your mind.

For those of us still learning, how do we work through the "Pardon my French" which doth so readily beset us? Wash our mouths out with soap? What lye destroys lies?

If I may but quote the wonderfully sage Mr. Thumper, rabbit: "If you can't say something nice, don't say nothing at all."

It's rough. Who walks around in silence? We all have opinions, and in many instances, we feel justified, especially when people do dumb things. And they do. All the time. And then, if those people happen to be in our family, watch out. That *South Pacific* "Happy Talk" flies right out the window.

So, what is the answer?

Perhaps the best resolution comes through scripture and by way of an author. Ecclesiastes 3 states there is a time and season for everything, including "a time to keep silence, and a time to speak." Dr. Seuss provides this counsel in *Oh The Places You'll Go*: "So be sure when you step, step with care and great tact and remember life's a great balancing act."

It's all about the when and how. We can share our ideas and do so respectively. That is how we "move mountains."

Thoughts on the Grapevine

"Hey! Psh pst pst psh pst pst blh!"

"Oooh! That's juicy! I've just got to tell such-and-such! She will die! Just die!"

Thus, the information was bruited throughout the village, and so concludes the days of our lives.

It's like telephone. Remember that game? Only by the time word got to the last person, it wasn't anything near how it started. There may or may not have been sabotage… this whispering softly and quickly other non-related words in distorted fashion to ensure kookier results. Not by me, of course. Noooooooooo, siree.

It was a fun game, and if it was played the same way in real life, we would have more laughs.

As adults, we change the rules.

And not always for the greater good.

Sometimes we like to perpetuate situations. We hear or see something (maybe online), and we think, "I should tell this person about that. They should know about this."

We forget a few factors: One, people have the right to express themselves. That is one of the advantages of being alive today. We are free.

Two, people are entitled to their feelings. Stuff happens, and not everyone is going to be happy about everything all the time. Sometimes they may be frustrated; sometimes they might get downright angry. In any case, they are allowed to feel how they feel without judgment or apology.

Third, people can handle their own business. Despite whether or not this person knows what another person said, we can leave it to the one to take care of it himself. Unless there's some sort of murder-suicide plot in the works, it is not our place to interfere. If what they said really is that bothersome, we can talk to them directly, not to the other party in question.

In gist, if what you want to pass along will make a circumstance worse, resist the temptation, and keep it to yourself – lest you become the bad guy.

In other words, don't perpetuate situations!

Hold Your Tongue

(A few more thoughts on the subject...)

"Oh, oh, oh... Have I got a story for you! You're never going to believe what happened! Even though this person knew about this and that, they still did such-and-such and then that person turned around and..."

"No!"

"Yes!"

"What did they do?"

We may never know.

For some reason, we like to bleat scandals here, there, and everywhere whenever we can. The more execrable, the better! It's way more interesting. Like the country songs of forever, we get obsessed with whose car is parked next door, if so-and-so got together, if so-and-so broke up, or if this person gained or lost 20 pounds within the last three days. Who needs to read *People?* We live it every day.

After all, what is life without the juicy bits? Who doesn't like a sensational story? It's why movies are so popular.

There is something to be said for Mr. Osteen's expression, "If you cannot be positive, then at least be quiet."

Gossip injures, causing deep emotional scars, and it aggravates situations. Most of the time it is untrue. It is always exaggerated and pretty much biased, if I do say so myself. Does anyone ever ask the person what happened? No one asked me.

Honestly, very few people want their business broadcast to the world and used as a constant reminder of their mistakes. If someone falls, he wants to feel as if getting up is a possibility.

He wants to know there is hope for change and those out there who care for him.

So, while it may be the struggle of a lifetime, let's make like Joey and keep some secrets to ourselves, respecting people's privacy and allowing them the opportunity to share their own news when (and if) they are ready.

The Heat is ~~On~~ Off

There has been an unfortunate, disturbing epidemic of violence as of late, with people going on the rampage in the name of some cause or reason.

Although these actions have moved gun control to the forefront of our debates, there are still greater issues embedded within these controversies: namely, anger and depression management. (After all, there are many responsible gun owners.)

Let's be real. Sometimes people are going to frustrate us. There are times we want to forgo civility, reach across the table, and "knock some sense" into a person. We want to rally in the name of justice, all in this effort to get the other person to understand our viewpoint.

Anger is a powerful emotion. As our minds race with inappropriate language, our hearts beat faster, getting the blood pumping and the heat rising. Our faces turn red; steam blows out our ears. If we don't put this indignation in check, we will enter the realm of irrational.

At the other end of the spectrum is depression, an equally dynamic emotion. Given the heartache life can bring, sometimes it is a struggle to maintain the hope needed to keep moving forward positively. Should we continue the spiral downward, we will lose all claims to sensibility.

In both cases, self-discipline is needed, along with some sort of healthy release in which to deal with these feelings.

Violence is never the answer! When hateful or despondent thoughts arise, we must find ways to discard, not entertain them. We must learn to step away and say to ourselves, "You know what? This is too much for me to handle right now. I can't think about this reasonably."

Then we must find a productive outlet in which to channel our rage or discouragement. Here are a few suggestions:
- Walk the dog.
- Paint a picture.
- Build a masterpiece.
- Do yardwork.
- Practice breathing exercises.
- Heat Peeps in the microwave for 10 seconds. (Extra tip: Write the problem on it with a Sharpie.)
- Meditate.
- Count to a hundred.
- Work out.
- Take a jog.
- Read a book.
- Deep clean the house.
- Watch online cat videos.
- Talk to someone.
- Go out and serve.
- Garden.
- Write.
- Play a game.
- Take the kids to the park.

Find whatever works best for you. If nothing curbs your spirits, seek counseling. Do not deal with these feelings alone.

Only when we are calm can we find a solution. There may not be an instant answer. We allow others the opportunity to do the right thing, and when they don't, we seek for peaceful alternatives. We appeal to the system.

In every instance, our solutions should lead to love and respect for our neighbors.

Although life has its challenges, we can taper our tempers and cheer our spirits. As we learn to discipline our emotions, we will be able to handle conflict in a harmonious, nonviolent way.

It's Better Unrehearsed

The other day I had an interesting experience. While waiting for the light to turn green, an elderly woman rear-ended me. When I stepped out of the car, instead of taking responsibility, the lady asked, "Why were you backing up?" Incredulous at such an absurd accusation, I responded, "I wasn't. My car was in drive, and my foot was on the brake. I did not shift gears as I was waiting to turn." She questioned, "Well, what happened?" With restrained indignation, I answered, "You hit me."

To my frustration, the lady did not apologize or even ask if I was alright. Not once did she admit to her mistake, and it angered me that she did not take responsibility.

Thankfully, both the car and I were fine, and I sped away with the reassurance that I would not have to deal with her again. In my assessment, I could only figure she was 1) too old to be out on the streets, 2) she needed a vehicle she could control (instead of a suburban), or 3) both of the above.

Later, I found myself thinking about what more I could have said, formulating what could have been "the perfect response."

As the situation replayed in my mind, my irritation was relit, not to mention intensified.

Suddenly, amidst all these thought processes came the epiphany: *It's better unrehearsed.*

Had I said any of these planned remarks that came to mind post-incident, no doubt I would have moved to a shameful level of disrespectful and mean. The situation may have accelerated out of control, and who knows what else could have happened?

Sometimes we are tempted to believe it wise to have a sarcastic retort or clever rejoinder for every 'enemy' that crosses our path.

But just as Joe F-O-X advised in *You've Got Mail*, "when you finally have the pleasure of saying the thing you mean to say at the moment you mean to say it, remorse inevitably follows."

It is because when that happens, we are not ourselves. At that point, we have become slaves to our temper.

While our impromptu reactions to situations may not be the best, perhaps they serve as a smokescreen to reduce the further catastrophe that could arise in these instances.

Let us do what we can to handle our unpleasant moments with grace, and save our practiced numbers for the stage.

Put a Rein on It

If there is any lesson we learn from the cruelty of Heathcliff, it is this: Anger is an emotion that, when unbridled, does tremendous damage.

Perhaps it seems justified because people do "stupid stuff" and the world is unfair. With Forrest Gump simplicity, I can attest, *Things happen.*

Before pulling out the tar and rails, there is another truth to consider: We are all different. Though we share the bond of humanity, each of us interprets what-have-you through individual lenses. In other words, my Picasso is not your Picasso.

That being said, in some cases, we may be perceiving slights or construing drama where none was intended. Thereafter comes this manifested indignation toward those we deem "guilty as charged."

Instead of jumping to pre-mature conclusions, we could try to get to know one another better. We might even find that we like each other.

Unless we are Lady Susan, those who know us – genuinely know us – are not usually offended by our actions. True friends understand our hearts; they trust our intentions. I can't remember the last time I had a tiff with any of my real friends.

Bottom line: If you want peace, put a rein on anger.

Imagine the construction that would happen.

SEEING WHAT IS

Ever gone somewhere with a billion people and felt entirely alone? It's horrible. It's this empty feeling – one that leaves you thinking you made no connection with anyone and are worse for having come. It is followed by depression and all sorts of ugly cries (AKA negative emotion).

Been there. Done that.

These feelings stem from unmet expectations. At the onset, there were hopeful thoughts that this would be the night. Somehow all would magically fall into place. You would make a new friend, and for sure, you would find the love of your life.

Then it wasn't there. And once again, you felt let down.

Let me ask you this, though: Did you notice anything else while you were there? How was the music? Was the food good? Did you laugh at all? How many people did you approach?

Like a horse with blinders, sometimes we spend so much time looking for something specific that we fail to notice everything else. Then we are overcome with disappointment, when this could have been prevented – at least in part. A chunk of this sentiment called loneliness falls on shoulders. We are responsible for how and how often we interact with others, make or receive calls, or visit friends.

Maybe if we allowed ourselves to simply enjoy moments for what they are and not what they could be, then we might circumvent these thoughts of permanent solitude. In plain English, see what is there, instead of what is not. Accentuate the positive. Yes, we all want picture perfect happily-ever-afters, but they will happen when they happen; we need not obsess over them.

BRICK BY BRICK HUBRIS

Imagine building a house – a really, teeny-tiny house. (Smaller than a miniature.)

It has four, brick walls that rise straight up around you and a simple dirt floor. The roof is also constructed of brick, and it lays flat across the top. There are no windows; there are no doors. Outside the ground is barren.

You have built this house with your own two hands, and you are exceptionally pleased with its turnout. Though it is only two-by-two feet wide and approximately your height, to you, it is a castle. It is unsurpassable in its framework and its beauty.

Piece-by-piece, brick-by-brick, you put each part into place, using extra mortar to ensure structural stability. It would take hard labor – or most likely, abysmal destruction and tragedy – to knock it down.

Su casa is invincible, having been built to last. Oh, and if there was a contest, hands down it would win.

If only other people could appreciate it for what it is.

Those crazies. They have tried to tell you. They have tried to sway you from your designs. They even wanted to argue about it! Thank goodness they walked away, letting you get the last word.

You're an open-minded person, but you couldn't listen to them. No way you could discuss this in a calm and reasonable manner. What did they know about anything? They're not experts.

They said you would become inaccessible, but you contended perfectly, "I don't need the intrusion." What you want is what you need! If you wanted company, you would make friends. You would welcome visitors, even newcomers.

Here, barricaded from the world and outside ideas, you have everything you ever envisioned. Certainly, you've got your pride!

The Purity Aromatic

There is nothing like walking down the cleaning aisle at the supermarket. Mmmmm…. that whiff of bleach, the scent of lemon pine. It is refreshing. Seriously, it is paradise.

Then we get to take the solvents home and use them in our houses. We remove the dirt from the carpet and the mold from the shower wall. The tough stains come out of the laundry; the grout returns to its natural color.

Every day is springtime in the living room.

There is the soap with all its glory. Combined with hot water, can we say heaven on earth? Bye-bye mud. Bye-bye body odor and three days' worth of sweat. With suds and a rinse, somehow the funk magically disappears down the drain.

And it feels sensational.

Cleanliness rocks!

Sometimes we underestimate its ability. We take for granted its effectiveness. Conveniently, we forget its protection (from bugs, rodents, and disease, to say the least).

And moral cleanliness? Why, we like to throw that out altogether… or at least poke fun.

Notwithstanding, there's nothing wrong with keeping untainted from the world. It takes serious hard work, but assuredly, it is doable to keep innocent (yet aware) of what surrounds us. Those old-fashioned values safeguard us from most of the heartache and suffering that come from indulgence.

In addition, this obedience to a higher law leads to an acute connection with the heavens. Our minds are unmottled; our spirits are free. Therefore, we are more receptive to certain truths: We are royalty, and we are remarkable.

Sometimes we may not look like it. Sometimes we might not smell like it. But when we get rid of the grime, we know that we are.

And it, too, feels sensational.

Dance, Dance, Yeah

In case you didn't know it, I love to dance! Whenever I hear that beat, I can't help but move my feet. I jam to the radio and the elevator. Cue the music, and my brain goes crazy for choreography.

This passion began as a youth, when leaders taught us teens how to two-step, waltz, and swing. No wonder I appreciate a strong male lead.

Having said that, have you ever showed up to a dance party when it is first starting? Imagine the scenario. Everyone is seated at a table or by the wall, waiting for the "Cupid Shuffle" to come on. Some are at the dessert bar grabbing a bite. Perhaps a person is already out there, but the attempt to "shake their groove thing" isn't really happening...

Now, recall those few occasions (very few, indeed) in which someone took initiative, went out on the floor, and started to dance. Without question the person is into the song and busting all kinds of moves. He has "It's My Life" flowing through his veins, and you can't help but want to join him because of the way he is having fun. Suddenly you detect movement, only to discover it is you, pushing aside the munchables to pirouette out of your chair.

My point in all of this is to be like that dancer and own who you are. Sometimes you may boogie alone. There will be times you are afraid no one understands you. But, as you keep jittering with determination, dancing confidently to your own beat, change will occur. Miracles will happen. Who knows? As a bonus, people may join you in cutting a few rugs.

Remember, there is no one else like you – not a single person with your DNA, physical appearance, mindset, experiences, education, fashion sense, etc. Even twins are different.

This means literally, you are one of a kind, and you have a unique gift to offer to the world.

And so, in all things, I hope you dance. Keep movin' and groovin' like no one is watching. Party on, my friend!

IN DUE TIME

Once I was late for a meeting…. Okay, okay, so it has happened more than once, but this particular time there were extenuating circumstances – really. My alarm didn't go off. It didn't, I promise. Around the apartment, I rushed to get ready, eat a quick breakfast, and get out the door. Amazingly enough, I made it to the meeting five minutes after the hour.

To the lady in charge, however, five minutes was unacceptable. One second was unacceptable. Her comment was, "If the Bridegroom had come, you would have missed the party. The doors would have been locked."

That was when I realized that we should do everything we can (within reason) to be where we are supposed to be on time.

It is like my theater teacher used to say, "Better late than never, but best never late."

Although it is bound to happen every so often, most lateness is preventable. It is a bad habit we can break by shaking up our routines and leaving the house a little earlier (with enough time to "change a flat tire," my stepfather would say.)

If you've ever listened to Dr. Phil, then you know he associates tardiness with arrogance; this mentality that "the party can't start until I get there" or "they should wait for me." (As if what we do is more important than what others do.) Therefore, to combat the problem, we must retrain ourselves to respect others and their time. We have to learn humility; otherwise, when activities are "pushed back a few minutes," we'll think that we can arrive later.

I know, I know… punctuality is a challenge, but it is not an impossible one. With a little discipline, we can conquer the clock and enjoy more of the party.

Fully Committed

Wouldn't it be something if you could lose 100 pounds by smashing your face full of cheesecake, ice cream, fried ice cream, and homemade strawberry cake? Oooh, and extra creamy whipped cream? And bread. Absolutely bread. Oprah is right about that. Forget proper portions and regular exercise. Bring on the calories, and let me remain a size 6.

Or, if you could vege for however long and still be sleepy at the end of the day? No need for activity. The chemicals in the brain would automatically change to induce tiredness.

That's not how it works, though, is it?

The first case requires strict attention to intake, and the second, movement.

We can claim we are dieting all we want, but if our hearts aren't into it, come weigh-in time, Bob Harper will know it. Don't think you can fool him. The scale is going to reveal that number.

Thus, if you want the benefit and blessing, you must be committed. If you want entire benefits and blessings, you must be fully committed. There's no way around it.

Typically this same idea transfers to matters of education, profession, and religion.

It's about being engaged. Shortcuts aren't going to make the difference. Cheaters really don't prosper. Expect the "A" when you have made the effort. Recognize advancement is affiliated with hard work. Peace is given as principles are adhered to every day.

What this comes down to is responsibility on our part. It's about being there more than in name or membership-only. It is about speaking words, and following them with action. Don't be casual. Get the most out of your education. Be the best professional you can be. Live your faith to its fullest. (And if you're trying to diet, swallow that kale and do those squats.)

Whatever it is, do it whole-heartedly, and you will reap positive results.

Those Blasted Little Things

The other day as I was working out, the video instructed I do these "Waist Twists." As I shifted back and forth from right to left... and back again... I couldn't help but wonder if these teeny movements were having any effect on my overall health, and if they were, in fact, toning my waist line. Turning from one side to the other, it didn't feel like it. It felt like I was bent over swaying in slow motion.

Honestly, it felt like I was wasting my time. Unquestionably, there were other, more effectual activities I could be doing. Why did I have to bother with this one?

Well, often, I have discovered, it is these little things that make all the difference. When added up over time, they come out ahead of many of the grandiose things we may try. Some of them even become habits, which is why we should never discount the smallest of actions. Never underestimate the outcome a tiny choice.

And so, while I may question the purpose of something, I will always do it. These itsy, seemingly insignificant tasks will ultimately contribute to the greater good.

Back to Basics

Oh, to be five years old again! To revert to a world where glue was edible, shirtsleeves acceptable, and you could catch grasshoppers to your heart's delight. Life seemed so simple then, albeit quite gross. With minimal responsibility and very few consequences, childhood was a happy season.

Now, life is no longer what it used to be. Like Wendy Darling, we grew up…. Right?

Because it does not have to be that way…

Despite the increase in obligation and accountability, we can have joy now.

It comes by putting those "what I wished I had learned in kindergarten" principles into use. Confucius said, "Life is really simple, but we insist on making it complicated." We do it when we compact our schedules or over-analyze situations. If we would but return to "elementary," my dear Watsons, or that KISS principle we so love, mysteries would be unveiled, and great things would happen (like Arthur Fry's accidental invention of the post-it note).

Noticing the little things, such as the tabs that keep the foil in place or the recall button, can also make a world of difference. Picture the person who smiled at you in the elevator or held open the door; the kid who shared his candy or the card he sent. Figuring out total sum of kindnesses that surround you will unveil a crazy amount of goodness happening in your life.

By Their Fruits

When it comes to gardening, I am a neophyte. After years of battling the sun, birds, bugs, worms, and correct pH levels, I have finally had some fruition. Believe me, it has been quite the process, and there is still much to learn, especially if I want to extend beyond sage and tomatoes. People make it look easy.

How thankful I am seeds match their produce, meaning rutabaga plants produce rutabagas and squash – squash.

How glad I am for taste and its quick indication whether a fruit is good or not. If the crop is bitter, something went wrong. Maybe the plant suffered heat stress or waterlog. And unfortunately, if it is like cucumbers, once the vine goes sour, the outcome is irreversible, signifying it will most likely stay that way.

You see, good plants produce good fruits.

In like manner, good people produce good works. What a wonderful concept.

If you want to know if a person is exceptional, notice what he does with his time. Even if he is shy, the by-products of behavior should manifest whether or not he is someone with whom you would want to associate (or, by the same token, if he would want to affiliate with you). It is evidenced in what Mother Teresa termed those "small acts with great love."

The same is true with any causes we may espouse. What are the offshoots and are they worthwhile? Do they inspire tenderness and appreciation? A litmus test will let you know.

Just as the harvest reveals its plants, so too do our works demonstrate our character. May we always bloom with that which is tasteful and Divine.

Keep It Clean, Folks

Oftentimes, as I attempt to jog past baby ducks and sunbathing turtles around the pond, Louie's voice enters my head and together we sing in uncommon harmony, "What a Wonderful World."

Truly, earth is a glorious place to live! Here we are blessed with a myriad of animals and plants and a variety of color, not to mention countless miracles and other phenomenon. If we were to "settle" for "just a piece of sky," life would still be sublime. We would behold comparable marvels and have equal opportunity to cultivate our corner of the world.

Be that as it may, not everyone appears to have the same reverence for what we have been given. Based on the litter found in creek beds, parking lots, and long stretches of highway, the ever-increasing amount thereon would suggest some are striving for a living reenactment of WALL-E, wishing to spend their days among massive heaps of garbage. For many, it is "no big deal" to toss pizza boxes and cigarette butts out the window or to throw junk mail on the ground. Believe me, I've seen it. And so, the problem compounds... At this rate, we are bound for gardens of garbage.

Quite frankly, these people are mistaken. With more than seven billion people on the planet, it most certainly matters!

It comes down to laziness. These people know where waste goes. They simply choose not to dispose of it properly. They would rather selfishly shirk responsibility than do what is right, because it's not convenient.

Now is the time to change!

This is the moment to join the fight to protect the world that has been given for us to share.

Should you need to generate motivation, spend time outside. Having enjoyable experiences in nature is a surefire way to increase love for the earth. From stargazing to white water rafting, picnicking to mountain climbing, the great outdoors has much to offer.

Next, be an example. Similar to the neighbor who surveys our alleyway once a week for runaways, so too, can we set a standard of caring with our initiative, thereby inspiring others to do likewise. With technology, we can post how fantastic these efforts made us feel. We can celebrate the more than 50 holidays that encourage us to go green. Additionally, we can educate those with whom we associate about the benefits of clean living and demonstrate ways to reduce and reuse.

The list is never-ending for the action that is ever-needed to make (and keep) the world a better place.

Now You See Me

In the day-to-day of life, there may be times you feel invisible, like a dead ringer for Caspar. Someone cuts you off; others ignore your conversation. You discover some are unresponsive, disregarding invitations and calls, and those who avoid all eye-contact whatsoever. Hey, you may even find yourself in the narrowest of hallways smashing ribcages with another without the least form of acknowledgment.

How could these people have missed you? You drive a Ford F650 and were decked out in neon (embracing the 80's child within), screaming-slash-singing "Like A Prayer" at the top of your lungs.

Guess Mindy Kaling was right... you *can* do anything...

Despite the treatment you may receive from others, however, you are not *The Invisible Man*. Their failure to realize how real and valuable you are as a human being does not diminish the specific contribution you have to make to society. Don't let the attitude of others vaporize your worth.

Sometimes people get so caught up in Rat Race of life they can't see past the end of their noses. (Whoosh! There goes Mr. Bean!) In this instance, it really isn't you, it is them. No need to go to radical lengths to make them see. Simply do what you should to "Find Explanations in Charity" (Flannery O'Connor) and trust that one day, after the nose job, they will have better vision.

Keep living your life as best you can, and abracadabra, you will appear.

An Honest Day's Labor

Oh, buddy, wouldn't it be something if we could get paid to do nothing? Talk about a dream. Sit down and presto! There's money in the bank. Stay home in PJs? Cha-ching! There's goes some more. Oh, what a life!

In the words of Cher, "As if!"

Listen, as picturesque as compensated loafing may sound, after a while, it would lose its ensorcellment. Eventually, it would get boring, and discontent would start a-brewing. Then, who knows what those idle hands would get into?

If we were zombies, this would be a different story. We could sit in one of those fully-equipped sofas and watch TV for hours without bothering to shower or brush our teeth.

But believe it or not, we were made to move and do (and definitely bathe). Instead of developing bedsores like some automaton, we were raised to follow our passions, take up interests, and develop our talents. It's how we find our worth.

If we were lucky, we were taught to appreciate the value of hard labor.

If we are wise, we understand the greatest joy comes in doing our jobs well.

This means our efforts are first-rate. No matter the job, we take pride in doing it. We show up on time and work diligently throughout the entire day, not boondoggle. We go beyond the list of responsibilities. If something needs to be done, we do it – no questions asked. When training is recommended, we register for it because we constantly seek improvement, whether it includes learning a language or mastering a technique. We know to turn off our phones, waiting until lunch or quittin' time to check them. We don't steal time by sleeping or taking extended breaks!

In short, we give an honest day's work to receive an honest day's pay.

The results? Complete satisfaction and a sense of accomplishment.

Nothing beats the feelings that come from having earned our money. Of course, balance is needed. As with anything, when you're lopsided, you're bound to have issues. If you're bored with what you do, find a new job.

Remember, nothing surpasses what comes when we put honor into our work and give our best selves.

Giving You the Best That I Got

Remember the last time you wanted your friend's saliva-filled, been-in-my-mouth-for-over-two-hours piece of gum? Or when you went to the store and begged for a stick of used deodorant? How about when you told the hotel not to change the sheets, had a craving for unwashed lettuce or the good ol' double-dip? Oh, buddy, hold me back...

Now, maybe you're thinking, "Sure. No big deal. It happened five minutes ago. Why do you ask?"

But more than likely, you are one of the many people on this planet who wants – and even demands – the very best. There are no shortcuts, shortchanges, or backwash allowed. Get rid of the toenail clippings. Forget about a turning inside-out!

We expect first-rate service and premium treatment.

The question is, do we reciprocate this same quality behavior in our dealings with others? Do we render outstanding service, giving the choicest part of ourselves?

To truly do so may require a sacrifice of time, money, and effort. It may require discipline to turn off the phone and remove other distractions. We might have to postpone personal matters and business ventures until later, finding a more appropriate time to undertake them.

There will be moments to feed and not be fed; there will be times to listen more and talk less. Make an assessment, along with any proper adjustments, and provide a whole-hearted commitment.

Remember, each person has value, and therefore, deserves the chief of what we have to offer.

Strive for excellence. Create meaningful moments. Aim for 100 % Satisfaction Guaranteed.

I Can Be Bothered

Rush, rush, rush. At times, we are in a hurry to get things done. With bills to pay and people to visit, we are all some sort of active.

We make time for it because such "busy"-ness is important to us.

But then, heaven forbid, some dude knocks off our groove! The chutzpa! Time is of the essence! How dare he disrupt the flow!

In these moments where we are forced to stop, let us ask ourselves, "Could this so-called 'inconvenience' be a blessing in disguise?"

Couldn't we all stand to be more selfless?

As humans, we tend to categorize. Subconsciously, we divide activities by preference and people by our standards of cool. And to a certain extent, that's okay. Indeed, like attracts like. It is normal to prefer some things to others, as it is to spend time with those who match us. Much like gravity, it is a natural pull.

This should not be, however, a benchmark for consideration, determining whether we participate here or form a friendship there. To some degree, all have these notable characteristics that merit the perceived 'nuisance': kindness, love, patience, and sincerity. There is potential everywhere.

When we take a moment to acquaint ourselves with the "uncool" – by maybe attending an event or returning a call – we allow ourselves opportunities to discover newfound passions and relationships – ones that may even last a lifetime.

And those... those are well worth the bother.

To Lead or Not to Lead

At some point during this earthly journey we call life, everyone will assume a position of leadership, whether as a CEO, church official, assistant, committee advisor, sorority president, team captain, or parent. The older you get, the more likely the odds, and with an alleged increase in wisdom, the more natural the possibility.

But to undertake these charges requires skills – and some are not second nature.

Effective leadership begins with example. If you want others to be on time, then you, too, must be on time – if not early. If you would like your staff to work hard, you must work hard, finding something productive to do. The vision starts with you. Double-standards are a surefire way to squelch motivation.

This kind of leadership inspires others. The best boss I ever had was there before everyone. She worked alongside the workers and was willing to do anything, including answer the phones! If it wasn't for the work itself (not my passion), I would have stayed because of her management.

To rise to this level of effectiveness, start by outlining your goals and the steps needed to accomplish them. From there choose your role. What will be your part – more specifically, your action? A bellwether does more than govern.

Next, delegate responsibility and trust others to do their jobs. Although it may be tempting to meddle, interfering with each piece of the process, you would be better to step in only when additional training is needed. Micro-managing breaks team confidence.

Once assignments have been given, allow reasonable time for completion, then follow-up.

For many, leadership is daunting, but it doesn't have to be. Practice these skills, and you are sure to have success in whatever your responsibility.

TAKING THUMBS OUT OF THE POT

Ever have those moments where you just want to tell someone how it is? The person is completely unaware, her hair done "Last Dragon style," and you feel it is your duty – no, your moral obligation – to show her "the way."

But what is "the way?" And is it the right way, or is it *your way*?

Think about it, because there is a difference.

For some reason, we have this constant need to meddle with everyone and everything. We make it our business to tell them how to run their business. It's our prerogative to ensure his opinion matches mine, and if it doesn't – alakazam, it's time to go all "wicked stepmother" on the situation. I hereby denounce you on Twitter, and write you up for unprofessionalism. That'll show you who's boss!

Now, does that seem right?

It sure doesn't sound like it to me.

It sounds more like a power-trip, doesn't it? Like someone can't handle another person's gravy. How dare he have a conflicting viewpoint? How could she make such a distinctive fashion choice? Why didn't they consult me?

The answer: Because it was NOT our concern. Sure, we all have opinions, and yes, we have the right to express them, but it is not our place to change everyone's direction so it matches ours. *Bruce Almighty* is a movie, not reality.

We all have different points of reference, and one does not necessarily transcend another. We can respect where people come from, as well as what has molded their points of view. We need not dismiss their wisdom so casually just because "it's not how we would do it."

There comes a time when we must leave people to their affairs, trusting they will use good judgment to take care of the situation. (And if they don't, by all means, we can still be kind.) Who says we need our thumb in every pot?

Again, leave others to navigate their own beaten path, because somewhere along that way they will find their happiness.

Step Into My Shoes

We've all heard the adage "Put yourself in my shoes," but how often have we walked that mile? If we have tested it, did we truly feel what the other person experiences step-by-step? Was it comfortable, or was it challenging?

As a result, do we understand one another better? Sometimes I wonder...

There have been more attacks as of late, physical and otherwise. In one case I witnessed, Person 1 censured Person 2 for online remarks. The original comments were complimentary in nature – basically, observances of positive actions that transpired during a meeting. Person 1, however, interpreted them as passive-aggressive criticism, though no ill will was intended. Having read what was posted, I am still baffled by this conclusion.

Had there been a switch-up, Person 1 would have understood the latter's point of view: With two ear surgeries and a temperamental hearing aid, Person 2 no longer hears with ears. More often than not, Person 2 hears with eyes; visual stimuli impact and heighten the quality of each experience these days.

So now, there are repercussions, which I hope can be overcome. It may take time.

In the future, should we wish to stamp out these types of misunderstandings, there has to be more than a simple "ooh and ah, I like your shoes." There must be a lace-up and steady stride (not sprint) down another's walkway to grasp her perspective.

WHOA! SLOW DOWN, BUDDY

One of the most impressive aspects about visiting Japan came from watching hundreds of people in "rush hour" dismount the train and form a nice, orderly line on the escalator to ascend to ground level. There was never pushing, nor a single cut in line. Not only did each person go to the end of the queue, but they all stood to the right of the stairway, just in case anyone should need to pass. No one did.

It was remarkable the consideration. It was striking the politesse.

What these people seemed to understand was Synergy 101. They knew if everyone put away the "Rush-rush-hurry-hurry-baby-come-to-me" mentality, then all could get to where they were going in a reasonable amount of time. There would be an unbroken fluidity thanks to their applied patience.

Yes, we all have a lot to do. It's like we Martha about with a never-ending list every day. We have places we ought to be. And yet, at the same token, does anyone get a kick out of traffic? Is fast food what we want for every meal? Does anyone truly prefer operating in a sleep-deprived state? How about dealing with the Wal-mart parking lot?

I'm going to venture out and say "No" to all the above. What a nightmare!

And so, the million-dollar question: Do we have the self-discipline to slow down?

We would be more effective in our projects and with each other if we would take a paced approach in life. We could improve our relationships and take better care of ourselves if we learned to manage our time wisely and leave a little earlier.

Maybe we could even eliminate a few items off our to-do list. After all, are they necessary? Will the world stop if everything doesn't get done? Are we going to hear about it on the six o'clock news? Hmmm... Again, I'm going to guess no.

Take care of what is most important and leave the rest for another day. Breathe, and apply that brake.

No Other Gods

Nothing parallels a person passionate about his work. There is something special about the way he commits to it and how highly he is engaged. It is refreshing to see such zeal, especially if it is for a worthwhile cause.

There is a difference, though, between zest and monomania.

One relishes an idea; the other is obsessed with it. One can maintain balance, while the other engages the extreme.

Whether it's Kelly or Carrie, we idolize people, things, and concepts. We worship the stars, and we are enraptured by politics. We follow fashion and trends. We fight for what's right.

To a certain extent, it's terrific. We need interests, and we deserve justice.

The problem comes when we have put this whomever or whatever on a tower we've built to the heavens. Our whole world – our complete train of thought – becomes fixated on placement. Are they high enough? Are they okay up there? Do they need a different pedestal? This one feels a little rocky. Nothing is going to harm them, right?

Never mind the tugs on our pantlegs or the truck barreling down the road toward us.

It's official: We have crossed from Regular Joe to Crazed Fan or Political Nut. Balance has been disproportioned; immoderation has set in.

In the frenzy, we have closed ourselves off to other ideas, allowing reason to go out the window. Relationships have fallen by the wayside; noble projects into the gutter. If we are not careful, hatred will entwine with our enthusiasm.

It's a delicate situation, keeping involved but not overpowered. To stay level, we must look upward for the Lord's revelation on matters, so no other fascinations will throw us off-center.

EVENING THE SCALES

Ever try to squeeze sand, rocks, and pebbles into a mason jar? It can work... but only if done in the order of rock, pebbles, sand.

It we want to fit it all in, we must prioritize. Big things first.

That is easier said than done. There are many things we need to do; there are different ways to fill our time. And sometimes, it feels excessive.

And yet, we need not freak out: All things are possible.

Think of a first-year college student. The person has registered for an ambitious 18 credit hours, not knowing that in each class the syllabus lists ten, five-page plus research papers and multiple exams over the course of the semester.

Altogether, it seems impossible, and suffocation descends upon the individual. At first the person thinks, "The only way I will be able to do this is if I lock myself in a room and study all the time. From this moment on, I must cut out all extracurricular activities. I can have no distractions."

Sounds a bit extreme, doesn't it? But isn't that always our initial reaction when we get overwhelmed?

Now the student takes a breath – a deep one – and starts to organize. Because she refuses to give into self-torture, she creates a detailed calendar, listing when and where to be at what times, along with every due date. She outlines, in specific increments, what to accomplish daily.

Slowly, the scales begin to re-equalize, and the panic is subdued.

While she knows there will be days where all does not go according to plan, it is fine because she will do her best and trust that somehow it will all work out. (And believe it or not, it does. After she completes her first semester, she knows she can do this!)

Meltdowns may happen, but they do not define us.

As students in the school of life, there is much to learn. We can handle all there is to do as we organize our time, work hard, and ask for help when needed. We finish tasks in a timely manner when we set long and short-range goals, learn to divide responsibility, and increase our flexibility – adjusting as appropriate.

Remember it is necessary, even imperative, to take regular breaks, especially to eat, sleep, exercise, and go to church. Don't underestimate the power of the 15-minute nap. Do not let the physical and spiritual selves go to waste. If something is important to you, it is important to the Lord, and He will help you to accomplish it.

Believe in yourself. You are capable of great things. Find that balance, and with firm footing, complete the impossible.

WHEN THE TIME FOR DECISION ARRIVES...

As I look out onto the driveway, which is now a thick slab of ice, I am reminded of how much I hate the cold and the importance of being prepared.

Being prepared was an overemphasized concept as a youth. Mary Poppins ain't got nothing... Whether it was a date or dinner, for each outing we were asked if we had money, shoes, an umbrella and/or poncho, First Aid kit, toothbrush, sewing needle, safety pin, blanket, and exact change to make a phone call, if needed.

The idea was to be ready for any emergency – that's right, *any* emergency – be it a run on cheese or a tornado. And while most days it was easier to stay home than attempt an "All systems go," the principle of preparation primed members of my family to handle bad dates, Y2K, 32 hours without electricity... you name it.

It is a crazy world, replete with natural disasters and other unknowns. Lest we be caught unaware, and heaven forbid ill-equipped to survive or care for our families, now is the time to organize ourselves. One day Chicken Little will be right.

Now, I am not suggesting we raid every store for duct tape and water to practice our audition for Hoarders. What I am stressing is the need to develop the mindset of an Eagle Scout: Have essentials ready, money set aside, and an established skill set, perchance of disaster.

That way, when the sky is falling, there is the calm reassurance, "Everything is going to be okay."

Building a Personal IRA

My mother always says, "You make time for what's important to you." Perhaps that is why the excuse "I'm busy" has always fallen on deaf ears.

Each of us has been given an equal amount of time, the same set number of days. How we allocate those minutes is our decision; hence, no one should ever feel short-changed.

To take control of your future, ask yourself a few questions: What do I hope to accomplish? Where do I want to be? What type of bonds do I wish to have with others?

I hope your answers accumulate respectable interest. Do they feel worthwhile?

Then, on your mark, set, start your planning. Budget energy and means to ensure optimal outcomes.

It's fine if you haven't figured everything out yet. Not everybody wants to be a doctor, and that's alright. The world stays balanced because we are inspired to pursue different paths and develop various relationships. Simply figure out where you want to go, so when the Cheshire cat asks, you have an answer.

"May the road rise to meet you; may the wind be always at your back," and may you be blessed with many happy returns on all your investments!

THE MAGIC OF MIDNIGHT

While I am not a fan of winter, I like the sense of wonder and fascination that accompanies it (and thankfully warms my heart). On New Year's, the fullness of its charm sets it as the clock strikes twelve and choruses of Auld Lang Syne fill the air. Sighs. I have a new start. This is another chance. Another year has come, and no matter what it brings, I can improve.

Perhaps that is why I love resolutions; they second my determination to be better. Resolutely, I resolve every year to develop in the following areas (see Luke 2:52):

- Mentally (wisdom)
- Physically (stature)
- Spiritually (favor with God)
- Socially (and man)

To ensure the balance between stretch and realization, I set two-to-three goals in each category. Beneath those, I outline specific steps I can take to progress toward fulfillment.

Here is an example from a couple years ago:

Read the complete works of William Shakespeare.
        o Read at least one to two scenes daily.
        o Take simple notes of characters and stories.

In all honesty, some days went better than others. Those king plays were a beast. Now, I can report I finished, and maybe in a few years, I will try them again. Maybe.

Bundled with resolutions and knee-high socks, I feel summery inside. My delight stems from pumpkin cider and the turn of a calendar page, held at a Cinderella moment, as we started the new year.

Self-Improvement 101

O January, January, the month in which we re-commit to new beginnings. I offer a few suggestions to achieve improvement goals (also great at birthdays).

Physical

- Park in the spot furthest from the store entrance.
- Find a secondary task to do while watching TV (IE folding laundry, sweeping the kitchen, lifting weights, walking on the treadmill).
- Learn a new sport.
- Try Wii tennis.
- Take 10 minutes each day to work on a small area of your house or yard.
- Set a limit to how much time you spend online.
- Invest in a water bottle, and carry it with you.
- Add fruit to your cereal.
- Try a new recipe once a week.
- Incorporate vitamins into your diet.
- Make and take your lunch to work.
- Post a food pyramid where you can see it often.

Spiritual

- Start each drive with a prayer.
- Download the scripture library to your phone.
- Have your favorite verse accessible (IE on a notecard or post-it note).
- Read a chapter or verse of scripture daily.
- Repeat promises/covenants while showering.
- Count your blessings before you go to sleep.
- Memorize your favorite hymn.
- Subscribe online to a group that posts uplifting messages.
- Keep a gratitude journal, or dedicate one prayer a day to offering thanks (no requests).

Mental

- Try doing a crossword, Sudoku, or puzzle each day.
- Check out a book at your local library.
- Start a book club.
- Take language lessons.
- Listen to a podcast.
- Read at least one news article online daily. Try it in a different language.
- Watch an instructional Youtube video.
- Memorize a passage of Shakespeare.
- Practice a skill or develop a new hobby.
- Try a new craft.
- Tour a museum or sculpture center.
- Act as an apprentice to someone you admire.

Social

- Attend a community event each month.
- Hold a weekly game night.
- Host dinner at your house on a regular basis.
- Call, email, or text someone you haven't in a while.
- Send a card to your grandma or another dear one.
- Start conversations in line at the grocery store or post office.
- Sign up for a class at a college, dance studio, or art store.
- Bake cookies for your neighbors.
- Go dancing when possible.

Work While You Wish

Well, it has been 30 some-odd years, and the Prize Patrol has yet to appear on my doorstep. Here I've watched the commercials forever. I know the song.

Really, I shouldn't be surprised; I never entered the contest. And as Ed McMahon used to say, "If you don't enter, you can't win."

I guess I was wishin' and hopin' à la Dusty Springfield they would make an exception. I am a good person – most deserving, if I do say so myself. How can they not know that? I could do a lot of good with a million-dollar paycheck.

The man of my dreams, whom I will randomly bump into later, could come along with me.

Alas, I haven't met him. Later has not arrived.

I am million-less maid.

Hmmm... perhaps the odds may never be in my favor...

In case there was a question... Of course, I jest! Truth be told, isn't this how we are? Like Skee-Lo, we spend a lot of time wishing. We request the impossible on stars and with candles, on campouts or in front of the mirror. We want miracles, and we want them now, preferably without breaking a sweat.

And so, as we blow across the cake, we wish (with an *Into the Woods* "more than anything") to have money or to find love. Perhaps we desire fame; maybe a new job. We hope for a change in situation. We long for people to understand us.

We wish.

And then we wish again.

Afterwards, we wait.

And wait some more. (My foot's tapping.)

Eventually, we reach the point of frustration because nothing has altered.

It makes sense. We made no effort. We didn't call. We never emailed. We didn't want to leave the house. We thought the Prize Patrol should just come to us.

Newsflash: Dreaming without works is dead.

Logically, shouldn't we work while we wish? That is, do our part to realize our dreams? We are adept individuals, capable of submitting applications, budgeting money, and learning to communicate. We can take initiative and meet people. It "makes no difference who you are." Use your skills to advance to satisfaction and beyond.

I think Ed would agree: Enter the lottery of a fulfilled life, and with continued application, work to win your million-dollar wish.

A Little Healthy Competition

There are times you just have to throw down the gauntlet and challenge a person to a rousing game of Monopoly at high-noon on a given day.

There are moments when you need to weave through billions of people to get that blue ribbon.

We want to go head-to-head. We long to play hard, because we crave the competition. We thrive on it. It is as if we yearn to heckle, boo, and 'talk smack' – especially if it ensures a victory.

Is that such a bad thing? Well, only if we lose our sportsmanship.

No doubt Ayn Rand would agree: Competition encourages us to be better than what we would otherwise be alone. There is something about corrival that pushes us to do our best; to get more creative; to refine technique. We work assiduously when we know we are up against someone or something, be it a classmate, a deadline, or better yet, a version of our past selves.

In these times of rivalry, we are taught how to be gracious winners and losers. We are prepared to handle those formidable struggles that may appear later in life.

Do we need ribbons for participation? No, not really. Showing up is only part of the victory. The real celebration comes from conquering the valuable lessons associated with taking part in these matches – win or lose.

Won't You Be My Neighbor?

The other day I met a new neighbor that lives on a street somewhat close to my house. As I walked by with my fur babies, she came outside with hers and introduced herself. Right away we became friends, and every time we see each other, we chat for a bit. My babies love her!

It's nice to know another amiable face – one that is real and in proximity.

In today's world that doesn't always happen. We travel every which way except to the houses around us. There is technology, which connects us to people in Mississippi and across the pond, and still we haven't met the guy next door. We may not even know what he looks like, just what he drives.

And yet, these people have names, and they have value. If we were to talk with them, we would discover they have interesting stories, similar dreams, and contributions, and they are but ten feet away!

Naturally, as we increase association, we will become more comfortable. We will build trust and start to look out for each other. Together we'll make the neighborhood a finer place – with or without the cardigan and sneakers.

Looking Past Appearances

A bishop once wanted to test the charity of his congregation. He dressed up as a pauper and stationed himself outside the church on a Sunday morning. Soon the members began to arrive, and to his dismay, almost every one of them ignored him. He waited until they had all entered the building before walking in and up to the pulpit. Weren't they surprised?!

As people, we have been created differently. Some of us have warts and moles in the most awkward of places. Some have quirky, somewhat offsetting personalities. We are at diverse stations in life. There are those who have fallen on hard times and have yet to recover, while others are riding high on success.

Regardless of how we look or where we are, we have this in common: We are human. And as humans, we need love; we need touch; we need care. We ache to feel valued. Sometimes we must ask for help.

It is easy to be nice at church (at least most of the time). Sure, we can share a pew.

But what happens when we step outside? Do we possess the same altruism? Are we able to look past appearances into the soul of another person? To recognize his or her worth, even with a grimy face and tattered cardboard?

It is about more than just money. It is recognizing the significance of a person, showing that you stand on equal ground.

Again, we have been made differently, and we stand in many places, but that shouldn't change how we treat one another.

Too Many Assumptions

Due to recent events between officers and civilians, a friend of mine took action by writing local authorities to express her concern and offer possible solutions. Her letter was thoughtful and articulate. Within the piece, she recalled past grievances she had experienced when dealing with those in authority because of her skin color.

What was most striking about her examples, though, was that I could relate. Interestingly, I have had some of the same experiences, only I did not attribute them to race but to someone who was having a bad day.

In another situation, a friend's co-worker was written up for not doing her job. She was fulfilling maybe two of fifteen job responsibilities. Instead of owning up to her indolence, this woman filed a complaint with the EEOC, which was immediately dismissed.

Finally, the other week, I listened as TV hosts commented on a critic's unfavorable review of a recent movie release. Even though none of them had seen the film (to have their own opinions), they were quick to conclude that this must be a case of "sexism." Online, many people posted both positive and negative reviews of the same picture in discussion after going to see it.

These examples are given by way of illustration. Today's world is quick to make assumptions, and quite frankly, we are making far too many of them. (Is that too much of an assumption?)

What ever happened to giving people the benefit of the doubt? To lingering on the side of charity? To taking responsibility and understanding differing viewpoints?

Sure and sadly, there are those who are racist, sexist, ageist, and what have you. We live in an imperfect world, which means there will always be those who have issues and cannot be nice.

But that's not everyone. There are many people in this world who are not like this, and sometimes those people have bad days. No one is foolproof to sin and temptation, and certainly no one handles everything well all the time. Sometimes it is a case of doing the best he can.

Rather than U-and-ME inferring the worst, let's see if we can find the real reasons behind a person's behavior. Let's research. Make observances. Don't speculate – ask questions. Get to know someone on a more profound level. Communicate. Express feelings with kindness, then listen – really listen – to the response. We might just be surprised at what we uncover.

In fact, if anything, we might learn "there is a broader picture than [our] own point of view" and find wisdom in limiting assumptions.

Beware the Cray

Perhaps this is a point upon which we can all agree: Today's world is not what it used to be.

With shootings, rampant accusations of alleged misconduct, and violent protests happening on a daily basis, along with body shaming, political upheaval, and those psychotic drivers who lay on the horn for two miles over perceived "slights," it doesn't feel much like "the best of times."

For the somewhat normal, it is like living with a bunch of crazy people... Or maybe they're normal, and we're crazy...

In any case, how will we survive? Do we opt for petty, en lieu of mature? Stoop to their level to fight back? Wish we were licensed to carry, or pray they get schooled?

There will always be possible "solutions" that come to mind...

But do any of them lead us to return grace for hate? Which of them remedy the problem in a constructive way? Are there those that would mend the situation?

If yes, then by all means, act.

If no, walk away. Wait until you have an idea that elevates. Act when you know it will improve relationships and change circumstances for the better. Do not step in anger or haste.

If nothing comes to mind, trust Someone Else will take care of it.

There is enough going on without us joining in on it. It is smart to be alert but wise to gauge our reactions. To change the world, we must learn to be more perspicacious.

Exclude-Me-Not

Never underestimate the power of an invitation. With a single "Please, come," you could change a person's entire world.

For beneath the simple invite is an underlying acceptance, a palpable remembrance of one's existence. Essentially, you are stating you like a person well enough to request his company – a high compliment, to say the least.

We can always enlarge our hearts and social circles to include one more person, even someone very different than us. There is no need to limit our coterie to the single or the wealthy, those with children or ones within our area. Sometimes we subconsciously blackball the odd man, and no one should feel as if she is in constant battle against the Plastics.

With today's technology, to practice inclusion is as smooth as ever; within seconds, we can send a text or create an event. We can calendar plans and have Siri send a reminder. It is that simple.

And so, before another person cries, "Hey, wait for me," let us open our arms and motion, "Please join me, my friend."

IN THE MUSH POT

To those of the shy persuasion:

If you are akin to Ambrose Monk, preferring home to the outside world, rest assured you are not alone.

It can be tough befriending strangers, to meet and greet those outside Stars Hollow. Some of us do better in groups of eight. We have our friends and loved ones, whom we have cursed with eternal longevity and an inability to move. Seemingly, that is all we need.

Why, therefore, put yourself out there to be subjected to discomfort?

Robert Putnam lists a myriad of reasons, ranging from health to democracy. In gist, being social is intertwined with our happiness. We may have entered the world alone, but we live life with others.

And so, take a deep breath and have that pep talk with the mirror. You can do this! By mustering an ounce of courage, you can get involved.

To start:

Set goals. Choose your activity level, be it once a month or twice a week. Determine how often you will attend functions and what you will do when there. Dare to participate, no matter how crazy it may seem.

Discover the art of chit chat. Introduce yourself to at least one person.

Deepen those laugh lines, and keep that smile on your face. There is some truth behind the adage "Fake it 'til you make it."

Finally, befriend an extrovert. Since their challenge is to promote inclusion, they will put you at ease while in the thick of interaction.

As you strip away reservation, may you be blessed with new rapports and an extended community. And who knows? With all your efforts, you just might win the Pan-Pacific Grand Prix.

Sincerely,

A Fellow Introvert

LOOK AT THAT BEAUTY

Everyone has his own standard of beauty. For some, good looks are associated with height and waistline; for others, the gauge is connected to confidence and poise.

At times, it would appear as though a few are considered handsome. Should the rest of us wish to near these 'benchmarks of beautiful,' some assembly would be required, such as the addition of heavy make-up or provocative dance moves, or for some, proposed surgery and a wardrobe overhaul.

The world is too diverse to have such a boxed ideal of appealing! In fact, the incredible variation in people would suggest an externally-based yardstick to be impossible.

For me and my house, attraction radiates from internal goodness. It blossoms from within and transcends beyond proportion, features, and skin type. It glitters under benevolence and magnanimity of soul. In truth, it is patterned after the Lord's method of evaluation, which "looketh on the heart" (1 Samuel 16:7)

What this means is beauty is beyond skin deep; it has tremendous depth.

If our hearts our pure, we will forever be aesthetically pleasing.

All or Nothing

One of the greatest attributes I appreciate about our nation is the freedom of speech. We use our brains to formulate ideas and our hearts emotion to create this beauty of expression. Moreover, we have the right to worship and believe how we so desire and allow all that same opportunity.

These days, when a person does something "wrong" – particularly, a prominent person – he is socially lynched and crucified without any recourse of redemption.

On an individual level, we understand we are human, and therefore, prone to make mistakes. When we err, we ask for mercy, and in most instances, it is given.

Broaden that to those in positions of power and somehow we forget that they, too, are human. They might put on more expensive pants one leg at a time, but they are still like us. They mess up. Pressure, or maybe sheer annoyance from constant scrutiny, might cause them to crack. Like any of the hoi polloi, they will suffer the consequences of their behavior. You can't pick up one end of the stick without picking up the other; it is the nature of the beast.

Now, don't get me wrong. Those in authority hold a responsibility to society. From movie stars to politicians, with the influence these people have and carry, they have been given a role of leadership, whether they like it or not. With this power comes "certain obligations."

So, yes, they do have a mantle to uphold.

However, for a nation that is trying to heal and re-unite despite rampant eristic issues, we are a bit harsh in our treatment of others – even extremist. It is especially evident in the detraction of those in the spotlight.

For example, a woman who behaves unmannerly has her music banished forever on radio. Amid unproved accusations, a man loses his legacy, and his reputation is permanently tarnished. A business owner states his beliefs, and his products are boycotted. Another one speaks impetuously and his network drops him. One guy made a blasphemous comparison and was assassinated.

Now, historic symbols that carry multiple meanings are being removed and statues marred because a few find them offensive. Down with Christmas and nativities.

Encouraged by this "mediassacre" all-or-nothing standard, we have brought this same attitude into our personal lives. Those with different opinions are shamed; others are called out with profanity and ridicule, with this pinpointing of the smallest of grammatical errors as a reason to invalidate their viewpoint. Many have been "un-friended," and there has been name-calling on every side.

None of these actions exhibit open-mindedness, love, or tolerance. Hate cannot, nor will it ever, bridge the gap between people.

Believe me, I understand reprimand when reprimand is due, and I know the frustration that comes from injustice. But can we not follow chastisement with an "increase of love?" (Doctrine & Covenants 121:43) Unless it is a grandiose act of treason or an action that endangers lives, we should be able to look past grievances. If we wish to see change, then at some point, we must extend a hand of forgiveness on both a self and societal level. Love is the great motivator.

Furthermore, there are certain truths we must understand:

- We are all allowed to have our own viewpoint. You have yours; I have mine – and they can be different.

- Everyone will not agree on everything.
- Some people may act in what we consider ignorance.
- Sometimes we will act ignorantly.
- There will be multiple, numerous times we mess up (sometimes inadvertently and other times stupidly).

Opposition will always exist. We live in a world of contrasts, which means there are trolls to our fairies, and ugly to our pretty. Notwithstanding, we can teach and lead the way through example. We can pardon offenses and use moderate means to handle situations, thus finding middle ground.

Finding Neutral Ground

What a peculiar world it would be if we all liked toasted peanut butter and banana sandwiches with honey, Cheerios, and a dash of cinnamon! I don't know about anyone else, but I would be elated. Talk about heaven on earth.

The reality is we have divergent tastes. It is next to impossible to find someone who feels the exact way you do about music and food, let alone those bigger matters, like religion and politics. We experience and process everything uniquely.

And guess what? That is acceptable.

Everyone is entitled to an opinion. Each is free to feel the way he feels, even if you don't understand the sentiment. If we talked solely with those whom we share the same viewpoint on every issue or have all things common, we would never get married, nor have any friends. It would be a very lonely existence.

Don't discount a person because he won't walk barefoot in the park. Learn to be tolerant until you figure out how to love. We would do well to repeat to ourselves, "Our ideas may be poles apart, but we can still respect one another." Choose to forgive; opt to compromise.

In many cases, should we wish to keep rapport, we must meet half-way, else there will be a lot of Princess Consuela Bananahammocks running around.

Bully for Him

It seems we have all met them: "Feminists... Intellectuals... Ugly people."

Today I add "unhappy-ists" to Miss Morningside's list. You know the type: the unsympathetic folk who roam our homes and neighborhoods, invade our workplaces and schools, sometimes our church buildings, with suppressed smiles and wrinkle-free complexions. For them, the x-number of years on earth have been ones of anhedonia and woe, hence the lack of sparkle and laugh lines.

At first, this misery appears to be due to some sort of chemical imbalance. Thereafter comes the rationale these people must struggle with serious health or family problems, or they have dealt with the residual effects of poor choices. For all you know, it's a case of "bad blood." They are upset because of an unyielding stance against their negativity. Maybe they are angry with God or with themselves.

Why else would they take pleasure in controlling situations and ignoring others? What would cause such despondency and a refusal to communicate? How did they become hateful, holding onto an unfounded grudge?

As outsiders, it is obvious: Their unhappiness overshadows their ability to be kind! Their bitterness withholds them from any form of love, any type of affability.

Still, such persons are to be pitied, not reviled. They deserve compassion, not retaliation. As disciples of Christ we have been commanded to love everyone, friendly and unpleasant alike, returning well in every instance of ill.

This is not always easy. In fact, it is never easy! Sheesh! But, as we increase in love toward our Heavenly Father, this will become manageable. It will be a natural flow of feeling from Him to the most carping, mean-spirited around us.

Remember, it is not our place to take matters into our own hands. We are to act in accordance with what we claim to believe, cherishing one another. Leave it to the Lord to counsel with the haters, the grumpy and the indifferent about their behavior.

Thus, "by this shall all men know that ye are my disciples, if ye have love one to another" (John 13:35).

Color-Coordinated

Brace yourself, here it comes: I am... not a fashionista.

Like most true Texans, I am comfortable going to Wal-Mart in my pajamas (not that I do, mind you... at least not too often).

I am what you would call ridiculously low-key. This doesn't mean I don't appreciate style. There is nothing like matching a red dress with gold earrings or off-setting a slick black dress with turquoise pumps and a chunky necklace. Who cares if the dress is white and gold or black and blue? I admire – even enjoy – the way individual pieces contribute to the whole of the ensemble. Each part has unique value, but together the contrasting threads intertwine to create something more beautiful.

Undoubtedly, it is the same with humans. We were designed to complement one another. Well could we sing, "We go together."

It is most unfortunate that many have suffered prejudice in some form or fashion. Discrimination is not exclusive to one set of individuals, and sadly, blatant manifestations of hatred continue today because of ignorance and flagitious choices.

So, what is a person to do? Clean out the closet and stick to one color? Never mix and match again?

The answer is a resounding NO!

Isolation is never the answer. The more we focus on specific colors, the more divided we will become. We need to understand, racism is not just "[insert color]'s" problem, it is a people problem.

To become united, we must view the accouterment as a whole; we must notice how every contribution enriches the totality of the attire. We must spotlight our commonalities. We are all children of God; therefore, we are brothers and sisters. Lest our neighbor be unaware, we need to share this information with him. Should he need milk, start at base level: We are all human beings. Said Shylock to Salarino and Solanio in Shakespeare's *The Merchant of Venice:*

"Hath not a Jew eyes? Hath not a Jew hands, organs, dimensions, senses, affections, passions? Fed with the same food, hurt with the same weapons, subject to the same diseases, heal'd by the same means, warm'd and cool'd by the same winter and summer, as a Christian is? If you prick us, do we not bleed? If you tickle us, do we not laugh? If you poison us, do we not die?" (Act III, Scene I)

Naturally, we can substitute "Jew" for any group of people.

If we have differing views, let us agree to disagree. If our opinions vary, let's express them tactfully or walk away. There is no reason why we cannot treat each other with love, kindness, and respect. In a similar vein, we shouldn't have to worry about "de-friendment" for stating a position. There are actual, feeling persons sitting behind those keyboards.

Let us step out in style as we appreciate each member of humanity and his addition to the outfit of society.

The Spice of Life

Once upon a time, in the not-so-distant past, a woman was turned away from an event because she was not a native speaker of the language in which the function was to be presented. Surprised at the exclusion, she pleaded for compromise: "Do as you wish! Speak that language, but provide translation, either by person or through a headset." Again, she was dismissed, with the brief explanation "that translation wouldn't be the same" and "obviously, you do not understand the reasons behind this decision." Her heart was saddened. She felt troubled. This woman knew she should be there, united with these individuals, acting as one.

Alas, the doors of rejection were closed on her and all others that were first taught to speak English.

Little did these organizers know, when they made their choice, a certain point was understood: This was not a question of language, but rather, it was an issue of racism.

If there is anything in which I am sure, it is we are the offspring of God. The Man in the Sky – He whom I call Father – created every individual who has been, is, and ever will be on this earth. Thus, we share the same Parentage; we have matching lineage.

Similar to our earthly mamas and papas, we have been asked to play nice one with another – to share our toys, to keep our hands and bodily functions to ourselves, and to be kind. In fact, we have been commanded to love each other (John 13:34).

Undoubtedly, this is not a piece of cake. Not only do we vary in color and language, but we differ in size, features, and personality. Clearly (and thankfully), our Father is a fan of variety.

Like a puzzle, we have to figure out how we work together. While this may appear daunting, it is not impossible. Just as a body needs its parts and a cake ingredients, so too, do we need each other. Together we create a full picture. Our individual contributions allow us to function, taste, and exemplify the full measure of beauty when we serve as one. If we continue strong in these efforts, exercising genuine warmth and welcome, we will achieve a unified ever after.

A Whole New World

Whether by plane, magic carpet, or favorite rocket ship, there is much to observe and explore in this world. Sandwiched between the beauty of nature and the history of man is the dazzling charm of mountains and gardens, waterfalls and castles, and much, much more.

Truly, the Lord has done a remarkable job, and under His inspiration, so has man.

Travel is well-worth the investment. There is a certain joy associated with visiting places – even within our own borders – that helps us as individuals better appreciate those outside our norm.

Somehow, and in some way, when we break from the comfort zone to the unturned area, our hearts change.

Perhaps because there is only so much you can excogitate inside the box. There is a limit to what you can do with that cardboard.

But outside… well, that's a different story. The possibilities for discovery are endless.

Unfortunately, with the problems of today, it is not always safe to get here and there, and thus, precaution is needed. In some cases, our visits may be restricted to a digital adventure, scouting with the eyes, not feet.

Not to worry – no matter how the travel is done, it will still serve to expand our horizons.

FRIENDS, FRIENNIES, FRENEMIES?

Once I was in this situation where I had to share an apartment. This girl and I were to work together as part of an assignment until directed otherwise. Because we had known each other previously, I was unconcerned; it felt like we would get along.

Everything seemed to start off okay. We went here, we went there with smiles on our faces.

Very shortly thereafter, things began to change. She started to nitpick, criticizing what I said in conversations and how I was driving (though it was she who had been in an accident). Next, it was sharing my personal information with others, even strangers – information I had requested she not disclose.

When I got sick one night, she sneered in frustration and disbelief. Unbeknownst to her, this was a condition that later had to be x-rayed and treated.

In another instance, she asked that I help prepare lunch. I sliced the cheese as instructed and put the pieces on the counter. Immediately, they were rejected. How dare I place them on a bacteria-infested counter, the very one I had cleaned that morning! Didn't I learn anything in school? Not to worry, she had. Everything was thrown into the trash and redone "properly."

There were comments... cruel comments... ones I would rather not remember but that are documented in my journals.

How grateful I am for one of the neighbors that lived next door. Every night as my "roomie" was getting ready for bed, I would stand on the balcony and breathe in this lady's counsel to remain patient and kind (the challenge of a lifetime).

Finally, in a last-ditch effort to bond, I shared one of my dreams with her. At first, she seemed supportive, almost encouraging...

until she decided that my dream should be her dream. "I'll take that prompting for myself." Months later, after we had parted ways, she called to tell me. I will never forget that conversation. My heart dropped as I picked up the receiver. I knew something was wrong before she started speaking. I knew it the minute the phone rang. Naturally, she wasn't sorry; there wasn't any semblance of remorse, only a disingenuous "I'll pray for you."

The glass vase pushed from the table. That day, she killed a part of my spirit, and I have spent years recovering. Thankfully, I still believe in God.

The irony is (at least to me) that she would tell others that we were the best of friends.

Now, maybe I am crazy. I know I can be weird. But, for whatever reason, my ideas on friendship are in contradistinction to hers. I don't know. I could be wrong. When everything came to a head, some people agreed with her. To her husband, who witnessed almost everything, it mattered none; integrity had no value to him, nor did I.

And yet, I have not had another experience like this. In every actual friendship that I have ever had, there is a deeply-embedded trust, respect, and genuine love - nothing akin to assisted suicide. There are no underlying thoughts of "I'm better than you." We want the best for each other; to help fulfill dreams, not squash them. It would never cross our minds to behave in such a belittling way. We would never intentionally hurt one another, and if we did, we would own up to it and make the situation right. Our friendship is not lip service.

Because this is my standard, something inside of me wants to hope that she and her husband have changed. Maybe they have; maybe they haven't. All the best in their endeavors. With glued shards, this is something I don't care to know.

Blast that Manipulation!

At times, it feels as if we live in a world where everyone wants to get ahead. Who doesn't want to find rainbow's end? Who doesn't vie for the entire package?

To a certain degree, we all want to be successful.

Sometimes, though, we pursue our dreams at the expense of another. We fix in our minds what we want, and so determined, we mow down any who stand in our way, not caring whether they make a recovery or not. After all, it didn't cost us anything, and there's always medication and therapy.

We think it's kismet. That armored car practically backed itself into our driveway. We ran into such-and-such haphazardly, so surely, it's meant to be.

But can we consider it a victory if we have acted cutthroat? Is it progress if it comes with far-reaching costs?

No, it isn't.

Sometimes we are placed in situations to see if we will do the right thing with the information we have been given. If we have molded a setting to ensure a particular outcome, then we have failed. We are nothing short of ruthless, using people and positions unfairly to influence results.

If a behavior eliminates another person's choice, it is wrong. Period. If the opposition gets no opportunity to present, then the result is a false conquest, which means at some point, it will collapse.

Also, we should be considerate of feelings. How we behave can affect another person's life for the better OR worse. We have the dexterity to minimize repercussions. In short, be honest. Deal justly. Experience natural, untainted achievement.

Give Me Liberty!

Remember the leg lamp in *A Christmas Story*? How Ralphie's dad was boggled by the artistic beauty of his major award and his mother not so much?

He put that tacky monstrosity in the front window for the entire world to see.

It was "cool," so it commanded attention.

Except not everything we think is great needs a display. Sometimes we have absurd thoughts that would be best left unshared – especially in a public forum.

Yes, we have the right to speak. It is one of the marvelous blessings of today to express ourselves without fear of punishment.

Lately, many have been abusing this privilege. It has been a contentious year. The mudslinging campaigns that flooded our nation nearly drowned us all. Those that got caught up in the process are still trying to emerge unscathed.

There has been an innumerable amount of hateful comments online. Unfriending has risen. Some don't even take the time to read what another has written. They skim, make a quick comment, and the disagreement escalates. Families had a hard time sitting down for dinner together over the holidays, if they met at all.

And this, all in the name of First Amendment rights.

What ever happened to "If you can't say something nice, don't say anything at all?" Have we come so far to have regressed so much? Where are our manners?

When did we get comfortable with tacky? Does Frasier need to give you "an etiquette lesson?"

In the quest to show off our leg lamps, we have pushed class aside. Somewhere in the "(w)rapping" – this overabundance of words – we lost tact and responsibility.

So now, what we need is a restoration of perspective. Find mom. Tell her we'll need her for the smash. Bye-bye lamp.

Nom Nom Nom

We all go through some rough years, but none seem quite as painful as... an election year.

Yes, that's right. Between the mudslinging and the poll updates, protests and daily analyses, every two to four years it is a dirty and stressful search to find the best candidates for governmental positions.

It starts in the primaries. The nominations are made... then come those commercials. Oh, boy.

None of these men and women are perfect, and none of them are going to appeal to every single person, given the range of diversity in our nation. Each has pros *and* cons. Maybe several... of both. (It makes me wonder if Presidency should be changed to one six-year term and Senators and Representatives limited to two terms.)

It comes down to the issues. We must study them out, and as agonizing as it may be, watch a few of the debates. The sole way to cut through the political mumbo jumbo to see who merits the vote – to figure out which person is the optimum choice, regardless of race, religion, gender, or political party – is by investigating.

This is not an easy process. With more emphasis today on verbal gunfire than topical discussion, it is a laborious task to find those key points of consideration. Wouldn't it be refreshing if candidates would say, "Let's put the character assassination aside and discuss what matters. Here are my plans and how I intend to carry them out." Scandal is only great as a TV show.

Now, we know with checks and balances, not everything would pass, but at least we would understand intention and focus. We would have an idea of where these candidates wish to lead us and if it is feasible to get there.

Truly, it is "Your Voice, Your Vote." Do your research, make your decision, and take it to the polls.

In the meantime, hang in there. Don't let this vexing political procedure eat away at you.

To Each His Turn

After watching the arduous U.S. presidential campaign, it seems safe to conclude that we have forgotten how to respect one another. Not only have the basics of conversation fallen into desuetude, we have abandoned the rules of debate. Of course, after a year of name calling, insults, rants, and Twitter hurls, that is to be expected.

Contentious campaigns = contentious results.

No wonder the nation is struggling to recover. This example of discord has been set by so-called leadership.

Remember when we were five? Those times we struggled with interaction, the teacher would intervene and remind us to "Play nice." We were taught to wait, allowing the other person to speak without interruption.

Apparently, the same standard isn't applied to adults.

Or is it? Methinks it has simply been disregarded.

True debate encapsulates politesse and refinement. Part of its purpose is to grant participants the opportunity to present a case in a formal, dignified way. It is a means of providing information to an audience to help them understand positions, so they can make a choice. In layman's terms, it is a coordinated conversation that gives way to open discussion.

A debate is not a forum for trading insults, nor is it a screaming match. It is not about having the perfect retort. There are no interruptions for "zingers." There should be no interruptions – period.

Each person is given a time to speak and a time to listen. If participants were wise, they would try to listen, not just wait to lambaste the opponent.

With the number of hot issues at hand and a desperate call for some sort of solution, we would do well to remember our manners. Then would we be able to bring polar ends together to rebuild what needs mending.

Heads and Tails

Have you ever searched for a one-sided Lincoln or a penny with a single obverse? Not easy to find. Not easy at all. If one does exist, it is as elusive as the Double Die Cent, if not more so. Every coin and bill has two sides.

Come to think of it, every dimensional object has a front and back, a top and bottom, and/or an inside and out. Whether it is posters or people, recliners or mirrors, each has (at least) two faces.

The same is true of every story: There are always multiple renditions, not one-way accounts.

While it is our natural tendency to present a sole version, there is always a flipside. (Just ask the wolf. He'll tell you about those piggies!) Something caused the behavior; an action led to that outcome. Before forming a definitive opinion, we need to take a meticulous assessment and investigate, like a Nancy-Drew-in-training. And even then, we must realize we may not gain a full understanding of the numerous cases worldwide.

Should we wish to develop our empathy, we could ask ourselves, "What would I have done in that position?" When faced with danger, an emergency, or the doggone obstinate, we can never be sure how we will respond. Indeed, we want to hope for the best, but let's be honest: Some handle stressful situations better than others.

In most matters, there is a shared responsibility of innocence and guilt; the percentages assigned to each party will differ.

Rather than quickly offering our two cents on social media or elsewhere, let us first make sense of what's happening and verify every angle. Thereafter, will we know what each story is worth.

Do Your Research

This may come as a shock – get ready to pull out those inhalers – but wouldn't you know? (Drumroll.) The Internet lies!

"What?!? No way! How can this be? I don't believe you! My world is shattered."

I kid you not. Not to worry, Santa is real.

In this time of political and social turmoil, people are rattling off random statistics and passing them as truth to support their claims. Pictures are photoshopped and statements taken out of context. Videos can be edited to show a partial picture, excluding what happened before or after a situation.

In some instances, almost have these online voices convinced me to do this or to believe that... almost.

But then I turn to truth – the unchanging, genuine, actual heart-of-the-matter – and I double, even triple-check, those so-called "facts." I go to the source; I listen to what the horse says. There are records of various data, as well as witnesses of what did or did not happen. (Let it be noted: One viewpoint does not paint a full picture).

Basically, it is all-out probe into what is real and what is not; an important investigation into every propaganda.

What it does is significant: it leads me to know how to vote, what to believe, and what causes to support.

Underlining point: Do your research.

The Religion Beat

Often, we are told and frequently reminded, "One bad apple spoils the bunch." And apparently, it is true. Fruits produce ethylene gas, which causes ripening. Overripening leads to mold and is followed by contamination.

There is a stark difference, however, between fruit and people.

One bad person does not, or at least one bad person should not, tarnish a group of individuals. Just because a person chooses to act inappropriately does not mean that everyone of that race, age, religion, or profession will do so. In other words, an individual is accountable for his actions (and his alone), and despite common stereotypes presented in media, not everyone is racist, irresponsible, radical, hateful, or dishonest.

As we interact with those of varying nationalities and backgrounds, we learn these truths:

- People are beautiful.
- All have something to contribute, should they choose to do so.
- And perhaps the most important, there are exemplary members of every creed and non-creed.

Instead of shunning an entire group – especially a religious sect – because of a person's actions, counteract with love. Just as we teach our children, we must learn to get along. How can we develop an actual relationship save we spend time one with another? How else can we foster trust?

We gain nothing by reacting in fear or by isolating our neighbor. United we stand, divided we fall.

We gain everything as we extend our hands in friendship and open our communication. Love heals.

Of course, we must always be precautious. Unfortunately, in today's world, there are many "ones" who make harmful choices. Sadly, they have been misled and mistakenly think they are justified, forgetting that anything that causes damage, impairment, or loss is wrong. So, yes, we must be smart and do what we can to protect ourselves, practicing general rules of safety, whether that be shopping at daybreak or reporting suspicious behavior.

Again, these safeguards are against those who engage in unlawful conduct, not groups of people. Although it can be difficult to separate the two, since our tendency is to lump them together into categories, it can be done.

As we strive to take positive action, no doubt we will see the remedial "fruits of our labor."

From the Horse's Mouth

Once, while sitting in the school library with one of my friends from church, another friend approached us to ask, "Hey, is it true that you guys believe that in heaven women are eternally pregnant?"

Without missing a beat, my friend responded, "Oh, yeah! Men too!"

Heaven is going to be very, very interesting…

I'm kidding! Before you freak out, let me assure (and reassure) you that we do NOT believe that women are forever pregnant in the hereafter (nor do we worship cheese, have horns, or sacrifice virgins). It is by no means doctrine – or close thereunto.

It's crazy what "facts" are out there floating around, as well as how much people accept without giving it a second thought.

If you want to know a person's faith – or anything he stands for – it is best to go straight to the source. If you want an accurate idea, ask a few that practice, given that people interpret adherence and application differently. They could provide official statements and resources, should there be any confusion.

There is no sense living in fear and discomfort. Many of the world's problems could be solved if we simply talked to each other honestly and directly, without taking offense. Most people are happy to share how they feel and could explain so-called "questionable ideology" in simple, relatable terms.

So, talk to Ed or whomever, and learn the truth.

The Knowledge Apprentice

It is amazing how much there is out there to learn! The world is filled with knowledge – so much so, it passes the point of incomprehensible.

With its vastness, there's no way we could grasp it all in one setting, much less one lifetime.

And so, we go from subject to subject, allowing our minds to retain precepts and random trivia. We try every day until death to gain something new. Then, suddenly, before we know it, *The New York Times* crossword is easier than ever... or close enough. (Hey, three answers! Woo-hoo!)

Probably the most fascinating part of the process is what happens when we make scholarship a quest, rather than a duty.

The more we attempt to learn, the more we grow to love learning. Somehow, we cultivate an insatiable desire to grasp as much as we can, taking Knowledge as our tutor. There's no denying the urge to read the dictionary, take a class, or watch an instructional video. We may even find a mentor or go back to school.

In addition, it becomes easier to learn. Whereas we may have struggled initially to memorize a small verse, now we can commit whole passages to memory. Finally, at ninety, we are the cognoscenti, able to recall additional dates and times without the supplemental Gingko. We can remember where we put our keys (which for some is a major feat).

In a nutshell: Our minds improve as we improve our minds.

Seek pearls of wisdom, and you'll find strands.

Use Your Smarts

Head down, I must admit, I have yet to figure out the Rubik's cube. For shame, I know. I could Google the how-to, except I would rather keep trying by myself.

You see, I like to use my smarts. I love to test my brain and gain knowledge, however meager it may be.

It is what I appreciate most about being human – having the ability to think and reason, improve and create, and attempt the near-impossible.

In some form or fashion, we all have these skills. We are blessed with capacities to understand the Washer Method, interpret Modern Art, and decipher the writings of Proust... at least to some extent, right? I may need to re-read that last one.

Even then, should we feel lacking, there are numerous paths to getting an education and cultivating our talents. It is our opportunity to pursue them and to make the most of ourselves.

Please note this is not a matter of comparison. While we may aspire to the intelligence of Mr. Rutter, we stand with a unique aptitude.

Remember, improvement begins with desire; it develops with effort. Use your brain, Pinky, and take over your world!

You Better Wake Up and...

Pay attention, says Whoopi. Otherwise, you might miss some important lessons, and there is a lot out there to learn.

Just when you think you know it all and are getting comfortable on the sofa in your PJs, something happens. You need a refill and a snack. Or, if it is life, you switch jobs, get married, and have four sets of twins.

Your routine changes. You enter a new division of training.

The cycle rotates back to student.

Suddenly, there is more to know. There is a myriad of questions, such as "What do I do?" and "How do I care for these other people?"

You want to be a good learner, so you come prepared with all the essentials, ready to take notes so you can do your tasks well.

But it is not that easy. There is dinner to make, cash to withdraw, and someone who keeps texting. How on earth can you learn amid this distraction?

Do you have the discipline to sit still? To focus? To listen?

Yes, there is a lot to do. There always will be. The older you get, the more responsibility you have. Sometimes it feels like there are no red lights.

And yet, if you wish to increase in knowledge, you have got to taper those wiggles to grasp key instruction.

When you are finally fidget-free, then you can get meaning from these new lessons.

UNDERSTANDING GREEK AND SUCH

Deep breath in. And out. Here it goes: I am... a kinesthetic learner. Ahhhhhhhh…..!

In short order, what this means is I am doer. I like to immerse myself in projects because I enjoy being busy. It is almost distressing for me to sit and do nothing. Maybe that's why I hardly ever go to the movies. When I watch TV, there is laundry to fold, puzzles to complete, and stitching to do. I can lift weights or walk on the treadmill. I want to see progress; I crave the results.

It can be tiresome, I know, but I love it! That is my life.

And you know what's really great? When other people notice. When they walk through the door, oohing and ahhing over these accomplishments. That's what makes me feel good.

You may not understand. This may be a real headscratcher. You might be thinking, "Seriously, who is this girl? We're both human. Supposedly, we speak the same language, but I don't understand."

Yeah. I get that a lot.

How ever will we get along? We'll have to move past Greek to studying squirrel. Squeak-squeakin-squeak-squeakity?

Have no fear. It is possible (the getting along... I'm not sure about the squirrel.)

It is about understanding emotional love. Apparently, we all speak and accept it differently. There are assessments out there, should you want an official color or love language. Many provide profound insight.

Regardless of whether you test or not, this comes down to knowing yourself, whether you are a peacemaker, or you appreciate hugs. Maybe you thrive on social interaction and like to futz away your time. You get a kick out of taking charge or being the life of the party.

You know you.

So now, it's time to get to know others.

What do they like? How do they interpret giving and receiving love? Is it the same, or is it different?

If it varies from your method, do you know what to do? Are you willing to compromise? (For example, I am willing to talk on the phone every once in a while for hours on end but not day-after-day.)

Most definitely, this will require some heart-to-heart conversations. The words should be there – just be sure you understand the definitions. To improve your relationships, you want to be certain you know – and can act on – the interpretation.

I Have Been Mistaken

Ever notice how you have changed over time?

I have. Physical aside, here is an internal observation: The older I get, the more Introverted I become.

I'm not sure exactly why that is, but I do have a few theories. The main one being I am tired of being misunderstood.

What's that, you ask?

I said misunderstood.

It has been said, "People who know my heart never have to question it."

How true that is! My family, my close friends – they know my desire for goodness. They understand my goals. Because of such, they never challenge or underestimate my motives. Whenever rumor is high around the mill, I can rest assured my character is intact. If they are uncertain about details, they ask. If they want to know more, they come directly to me. Never will they soil my name or hurt my feelings. Very rare – virtually non-existent – are arguments.

How grateful I am for them!

The problem comes when others do not take such time to find the true me. In lieu of the above, they draw their own conclusions. In times of needed censure, some have chosen anger instead of responsibility. They have pushed back blame, when really, they were in the wrong. Some have become quite the fabulist, spreading all sorts of falsehoods.

When these situations occur, it makes it difficult to open the heart to new friendships. It takes considerable effort to imagine the best.

Not everyone is bad, though. There are many people in the world with beautiful hearts, and there are several that are worth knowing. Be chary, not dismissive.

Make sure to try, for there is nothing like being misunderstood.

MASTER AND CAPTAIN

Recently, there was a revival of one of my all-time favorite shows. As I sat down to watch, I was excited. This is what I had been waiting for, and it felt like it had taken forever. I was ready. I couldn't wait to get started.

Little did I know, my excitement would be short-lived; my enchantment vanquished.

As the episodes progressed, I found myself more and more frustrated, and with the culmination, I was beyond disappointed. I have not watched it since.

Almost all the characters grew up to duplicate the mistakes of their parents. If mom and dad had a nasty divorce, she did too. If papa was a womanizer, son was likewise. If mom got pregnant unprepared and out-of-wedlock, so did daughter. If he or she settled into a job instead of living out a dream, the next generation followed suit.

In the original series, they all had this incredible potential. They were taught to be different. They grasped the consequences from this kind of behavior. They were educated more than most.

With these final outcomes, it was as if the underlying message was, "No matter how hard you try, no matter how bright you are, this is your destiny."

That simply isn't true.

We are not doomed to repeat parental gaffes. It's not one depressing eternal cycle. Destiny is not a set outcome; it is an achievement from choice.

While, yes, life hands out many a curveball, some things are avoidable. Others are surmountable. We are blessed with the ability to reason and choose our path. We pick what we want off the platter. We can write our own endings.

In many instances, we will have to exercise discipline, but if we are determined, it can be done.

As masters of fate, captains of the future, our decisions decree what will be. This means, if we like, we can replicate other parental doings... like their successes.

ALL BY MYSELF

There is a stark contrast between dependence and interdependence. The first is unable to function alone, and therefore relies completely on the charity of others, whereas the second indicates a mutual reliance between independent individuals.

Naturally, when we are born, we start as dependents, counting on parents, grandparents, and uncles twice removed to fulfill our needs. As we grow, we are taught certain skills, all designed to shape us into autonomous adults, able to prepare food, handle finances, and figure out transportation without having to ask someone repeatedly. (If, by chance, we don't know how to do these things, this is a great time to learn!)

Sure, there will be obstacles. What would life be without its challenges? People will lose jobs, change family situations, or sadly become handicap. There will be times we must ask for assistance to get through. There may be periods dedicated to "getting back on our feet."

This does not mean we stop being resourceful. Set-backs are temporary, intended only to be transitory stations in life's journey.

We were not designed to become permanent impositions. We were made to work; to fend for ourselves. Even those in nursing homes are encouraged to never give up; to participate in activities and enroll in physical therapy, which sometimes might feel near impossible. My uncle, who now has limited physical ability, is my hero. Every day he tries to do what he can.

There is something remarkable about self-reliance. It bolsters confidence, enlarges capability, and improves self-esteem. It wards off expectation and permanent dependency. It helps us push forward through the most onerous of circumstances, thereby allowing us to stand free on our own.

Being Your Own Person

To everything there is a season, a purpose under heaven, including a time to be together and a time to stand alone.

Sometimes we would rather one continuous season, such as an airy, prolonged Spring or a colorful, fabulous Fall. The temperatures are perfect. We don't have to worry about sweating through shirts with that blasted humidity.

But there is a reason for every season, whether it's to diminish the population of pesky, little gnats or help our bodies produce more Vitamin D.

So, too, does being alone have rationale.

While, yes, it is wonderful to have and be with someone, we must be able to function as an individual. It is imperative we grasp how to take care of ourselves emotionally, financially, and spiritually. We should figure out how to be independent, should there be death or illness down the road.

Moreover, it is vital we be as close as possible to a whole, healthy person to contribute fully to any relationship. Rather than jump from one person to the next, it is requisite we first work through and let go of past pain and heartache. Let yourself heal. This is a process.

In relationships, there will be times you carry the other person. This requires tremendous strength. You or your significant other may get down on hard times. This problem will be amplified if you are not complete. No one can carry someone all the time. In a literal sense, it would be overwhelming, breaking the back and weakening the arms.

In gist, aim for a beautiful interdependence, not a draining co-dependence. When the opportunity of solitude presents itself, maximize its benefit. Don't be afraid to stand by yourself. After all, no matter how long it seems, it's like any season – only temporary.

I.D.'s THE LIMIT

Imagine a world with only green lights. Wouldn't that be amazing? You could drive for hours on end and never wait or worry about getting your brakes fixed. What a dream – to move without limitations!

Or what a nightmare!

If we were all given a "go," the result would be nothing short of a headache from endless traffic and countless collisions. Unless you are some sort of anomaly, sitting in a car for an extensive amount of time, unable to return home to eat, sleep, or use the bathroom, is not that appealing.

Even if you were the only one on the road, tiredness or an empty gas tank would eventually catch up to you.

Thus, in some ways, we can conclude that we need constraints. We must have parameters if we each wish to get to where we want to go without major damage.

We require contrast. If all work and no play can change Jack, certainly an all-stations-go (or no) on life's highway can transform us. Ever met an extremist?

If we try hard (or if we're lucky), perhaps we can find some sort of balance between the opposites. Amidst the light and darkness, the hot and cold, and the sweet and sour, we can figure out what we like and why.

We can find our identity.

No more of "pan-"everything. There we have found preferences; we have discovered our mind! We understand who we are and how to think. We know what we believe. We have definition.

And with these developed specifics that both liberate and restrain as needed, we will continue to move forward to our destinations, even when we are stopped.

Craving Niceties

Man, the grass does tend to look more vibrant over there, especially when we are craving niceties, like a bigger house, a cooler car, or more money in the bank.

And you know what? It's okay to look and appreciate the color. There is nothing wrong with aspiring for a fuller life. It is good to dream the most impossible of dreams.

But what about the things we already have? Do we want our current possessions – or at least, do we want to want them – or are we so fixated on Buzz that we've forgotten Woody in the corner?

Because the truth is we all have plenty of nice things – that is, we would if we took better care of them. Those shirts from seventh grade? Still good. Toothbrush? Oh, yeah.

If we want to keep our belongings, we must tend to them. Outside of the Roomba, there don't seem to be any automatic, self-moving anything. It is up to people to cut the lawn and clean the bathtub. Dishes must be loaded into a dishwasher.

So why not go the extra mile to keep items in good condition? Why not move the phone away from that glass of water or put the tools back where they belong? Why not teach your children to do likewise?

Sure, sometimes it's a pain (Does anybody really enjoy ironing?), but consideration for what we have brings an added satisfaction – this ability to count current blessings, along with a longer lifespan for said objects.

Going for mint is worth it. As we take time to attend to our current belongings, we will find that we are already swimming in a pool of luxury.

Romancing Wrong

Normally, I am not one for television. Give me a good book or a ball of yarn any day, and I can amuse myself for hours, if not longer. But a few months ago, there was a new show that caught my eye. The premise was enticing, with a seemingly perfect balance between danger and romance. As a romantic at heart, I started to watch and found that it lived up to my expectations.

That is, until episode three...

Mid-show there was a scene that was somewhat disturbing. Although I had previously been exposed to something similar, this time it bothered me.

I had to turn it off and take a step back. Why was it so troubling?

The answer came: Because it was showcasing wrong in the most beautiful of ways. It was "normalizing" an action without the slightest bit of conscience, as if those involved were justified because they deserved it.

Whoa. This went beyond Leverage, past Ocean's 11, and into a new dimension, where I didn't want to root for the "bad" guy. Try as I may, I simply could not rationalize the behavior, and I did not finish the series.

No matter how we wine, dine, or dress it up to the audience, there is a distinction between right and wrong. And even though entertainment is just entertainment, there is a need to safeguard our ability to discern between truth and error, lest these "intriguing storylines" transfer into our reality.

Talk about a bad romance.

Let's Talk About It Now

If dating is a means to marriage, and marriage is the ultimate challenge, then when dating, it would be wise to bring up specific topics, so once knotted, it is a more pleasant experience.

That is to say, in the courtin' process, balance sweet romance with a bit of realism.

Rose-colored glasses are fashionable and all, but as Benjamin Franklin said, "Keep your eyes open before marriage and half shut afterwards."

What this means is when you get to the point of serious, make sure you and yours are in accord on matters of uppermost importance. This could include, but is not limited to: number of children, how to raise those children, where to live, who should work, money and spending, education, and any other expectations you may have. If the thought of ever having leftovers makes you queasy, talk about it now.

Understand that after you are married, all may not go according to plan. This shouldn't be a huge surprise. Since when has life been a perfect flow of events? An essential component of marriage is flexibility – this ability to adapt to whatever situation presents itself.

For now, you have a starting point; an honest idea of what you both want, must have, and can't live without. Later you can vie for some sort of compromise... or overlook the rest.

Perhaps putting it all out on the table beforehand will minimize some of those marital scrapes.

A Dating Do

How people find and marry each other is nothing short of a miracle!

You wouldn't think it'd be that complicated, given the number of people on the planet. More people means increased odds of finding the right person. Online dating is said to facilitate the sorting process. Supposedly one swipe equals another step closer to marital bliss.

And yet, how we struggle! Seriously, the struggle is real. It's like going to the supermarket to find cold medicine. Why are there so many choices? Give me three, people!

There has to be a better way, and it is bound to take more than reading someone else's bio. It requires availability; this idea of being open to new experiences and possibilities. Maybe a few set-ups.

Then there's the matter of what to do when on the date. For most of the world, it's a question of bar or barista. There's not much space for the non-drinker, unless milk or hot chocolate are available.

Sure, there's always dinner and a movie, but for some, that can be a long, drawn-out affair, since within minutes, we know whether we want to pursue a relationship with someone. Plus, you can't talk during a movie.

In the interest of time and sanity, why not cut to the chase and opt for something as basic as, let's say, dessert? Why not try a dessert date?

Dessert is the best part of the menu anyway. It's just underappreciated. By the time appetizers and entrees are finished, our stomachs are too full. Stand up, and we are at wading point. Once again, the caramel molten lava cake is postponed to another day. Sadness!

Why must this be? Can we not enjoy short, relatively painless encounters while concurrently satisfying a sweet tooth? Yes, it would be nice to take 15 to 30 minutes to dig into dessert with someone.

Then, if things go well, there's always dinner.

THE BLIND SPOT
(YES, ANOTHER ONE...)

Despite 2,500+ online dating websites, thousands of clubs, and regular church activities, it can be challenging, if not painful, to meet someone you'd like to consider the love of your life. It takes far more than a swipe or drink to find a near-perfect match.

Dating is difficult.

It has been said that the best connections come through mutual friends. But blind dates can be daunting, especially if that stranger jumped into the pool naked following dinner that one time. (I'm still recovering...) The aftereffect may be a slight hesitation to re-enter that world. Loneliness might be the better option, if all you see is that bare bottom floating into the horizon.

Hence the conundrum: If you don't try, how can you meet someone?

Maybe the answer comes with compromise.

Too often when friends play matchmaker, their intro goes something like this: "I have this guy I'd like you to meet. He's great, but he does have this <u>foul, unbreakable habit</u>. Would you be okay if he is into <u>this weird activity</u>?"

Sort of zaps all appeal out of it, doesn't it? As set-ees, we are not looking to "fix" or "deal with" someone. We are wanting to find the person "of our dreams" or as close as possible. We all deserve the best, which includes a positive preface before the initial set-up.

So, how about we make it easier for our well-meaning set-ers by offering one or two simple ground rules?

That is: *If you would not consider dating him/her (if you were single), please do not recommend him/her. Suggest only those who would (strongly) complement me.*

In this way, the middlemen act with reason, and the dat-ees stay open, while protecting themselves from additional uncomfortable, disappointing experiences.

It is true that the likelihood of finding companionship rises as we make ourselves available; however, it is fair to approach dating and its prospects with heightened vision.

THE HE-SHE PHENOMENON
(LAST ONE, I PROMISE.)

Oh, the magic of cinema! It makes finding love look easy! Girl meets boy, and instantly, the two share a connection and a mutual attraction. All of a sudden, they're at the same obscure places, sharing special moments. She plays the fool by tripping over everything, and somehow, he saves the day. He turns into an alien, and together they surmount some sort of obstacle, et voilà, they embrace as "Ah, Sweet Mystery of Life" fills the background. (Or something like that...)

Or, in modern speak, he gets down by the hot tub and asks, "Will you accept this final rose?"

In life, the challenge of dating is much more trying.

For example, you find someone promising with whom you share similar interests, only to discover an emotional mismatch. You have conflicting life goals and clashing humors. There is a dependency issue. The person does not reciprocate the same bubbly enthusiasm you share for him. In an angel/devil paradox, a mini-Greg Behrendt appears on your shoulder and whispers, "He's just not into you! Move on!"

It's a magical, complicated 'game,' says the world... but dating need not be such a labyrinth.

If you like someone, tell him. Gently. You don't want to freak him out. If he doesn't return the sentiment, proceed forward to another possibility. Don't stop to memorize his Linked-In profile or flip through the Facebook albums. That only bolsters infatuation. Those may provide insights into a person, but they aren't the same as getting to know someone. A picture does not reveal traffic behavior, desire for kids, sense of humor, treatment toward the elderly, depth of faith, or good sportsmanship, to name a few.

If you have a set covey of friends, try dating someone in it. Truth be told, you marry someone with whom you spend time. If you aren't interested in anyone in that crowd, consider branching out and talking to other people. Take a dance class. Join a sport. Host a barbeque or a swim party.

There should be a balance between taking initiative and allowing things to happen naturally. Don't complain you're not married if you are unwilling to try. You have zero to lose by dialing that number. At the same token, stay calm. There's nothing scarier than someone who is marriage-hungry. People in China can feel that vibe.

Much more on the subject could be said. To put it simply, you deserve someone who gets excited at the very thought of you; a best friend with whom you can share the highs and lows of life. Do your part to put yourself out there, and keep moving until you find that proverbial match.

THE ROOT OF ALL HEARTACHE

Once there was a girl who met a boy, and for a moment, it seemed romance would blossom.

The two texted back and forth throughout the day. When he called, they would talk for hours. She sent him a box of goodies for his birthday; he ordered her random gifts, even sent flowers to her mother.

He gave his heart freely; she was more reserved.

They had plenty in common, like music and interests, humor and intelligence. They talked of traveling the world and settling down. They laughed; they had fun.

Everything seemed ideal.

The problem was he was married.

Well, separated, and on his way to divorce. Only he hadn't filed, and when he did get around to doing so, it would be almost six months before it processed, if not longer.

The girl slammed on the brakes. If they kept this pace, talk of marriage would be on the table within the week, and that was clearly an impossibility.

He said he understood. Of course, they could be friends. He still needed to work through the issues from his ruptured marriage.

Secretly, though, he wanted it to continue, texting something whenever he could, however pithy. He wanted her to wait, no matter how long.

She toned it down, and he was offended. When it stopped going to his plan, he became upset.

Eventually, he threw it away – the memories and the friendship. It was Hobson's choice: If he couldn't have it, he wanted none.

They never spoke again.

And all because of unfair expectations.

How often have we made equally unrealistic demands? From "gluten-free, organic" everything to the perfect Pinterest re-creation, we hold a high bar for ourselves and others to jump over.

When no one meets the grade, we are disappointed. We had presumed the fantasy would be filled.

But the truth is the gauge was too high in the first place; it was beyond anyone's reach. People could duct-tape poles together and never come close to such an idealistic impossibility.

It is one thing to have standards. It is another to have nonsensical ones.

The time has come to reassess benchmarks and rewrite criterion. By all means, keep dreaming. Just remember to accept reality, if you want a happy ending.

The Great Switcharoo

"I love you. I really do."

"Then why'd you set my couch on fire?"

"It was an expression of my love."

"And the piñata?"

"That old thing?"

"It looks just like me."

"It sure does, doesn't it? Huh."

"And what about the burning in effigy? What was that for?"

"Because I care."

"I see. And let me guess… the mysterious package, the boycott, the slash in my tires – those, too, were tokens of your affection?"

"That is correct."

"Interesting."

"Is it? Is it really? Because you know how I feel."

"Yes, I do. But I feel differently."

"And that's okay. I'm fine with you thinking differently than I do. I'm very open-minded."

"Okay…"

"But don't expect me to stop criticizing your every move. And don't you think I'll stop the petition."

"No, of course not."

"And I'll have to unfriend you at some point."

"Naturally."

"Oh, and I may have to jump you in the parking lot after work."

"I would expect nothing less."

"Or perhaps the mall would be better?"

"Whatever works best for you."

"Is three o'clock okay?"

"It's as good a time as any."

"Wonderful."

"Is there anything else?"

"Yes. I'm going to marry that boy you like."

"What?"

"Don't worry. I won't tell him about your feelings. You'll never have a chance."

"Gee, thanks."

"No problemo! Aren't I the greatest? I couldn't be happy if you were happy... Ah, I just love *love*, don't you?"

1 Corinthians 13

AND LOVE, TRUE LOVE

Time and again, people argue, "If you loved me, you would accept me for who I am. You would love me unconditionally."

Talk about cringeworthy. Shudder galore.

Unconditional love is not accepting inappropriate behaviors. As a matter of fact, by affixing this "approval" mandate, the other person is placing his own provision on care – the very thing he is condemning.

Unconditional love is loving someone *despite* inappropriate behaviors. Like it or not, there are some acts that are unacceptable, be they spiritually or legally wrong. If the new relationship is that important, end the other one. If it means that much, work hard to earn the money honestly.

Don't ask another person to lower his standards because you want an endorsement. Don't accuse them of enmity based on a need to have ratification.

Nowhere in their rebuke was the message "I hate you" but rather, "I hate what you are doing." What a huge difference! This implies an ample concern for the other's well-being, as well as confidence in the relationship. They feel comfortable enough to talk to you about it in the first place.

So, give them some credit, and try to see the matter from their point of view. Clearly, they want what's best for you – and that, my friend, is love, true love.

Say Something

There is a story of a man who, in the early stages of his marriage, complimented his wife on what he liked about her cooking. Now, at the time, her skills weren't all that fabulous, but he made it a point to accentuate the positive and to eat all that was placed before him. Subsequently, she felt inspired to keep practicing, and today she owns her own catering business.

In another case, there was a man who struggled a long time with tact. No matter how hard he tried, he couldn't express himself without offending almost everyone. His wife stayed by his side and helped him with refinement. When he would err, she would gently urge him to apologize. Today, though a few issues remain, he makes and keeps friends better than he did before.

Au contraire, there was a woman looking for domination, no matter the cost. She promoted prejudice and dissension, hurting several people in the process – particularly youth. Her husband could have stopped her. Instead, he gave her carte blanche, allowing her to carry it to the extremes. Even after the damage was done, he still did nothing.

There was an engaged man that excused his fiancée's inappropriate behavior with a "Well, I love her. I'm still going to marry her." Perhaps in his eyes, loyalty superseded the needed reproach.

And yet, part of love is saying the hard stuff. It is kindly and respectfully putting into words what needs improvement. We address the problem(s); we search for solutions. Next, we galvanize into action, lending a hand if necessary.

There is never a cause to be rude. There is nothing to gain from being spineless. (If anything, the issue will get worse.) So much weight is in the approach.

We are here to make each other better. It is one of the major components of being a couple; of having a family. We discern weaknesses and do what we can to strengthen them. We are each other's cheerleaders!

Let's pull one another onto higher ground.

Marriage Matters

Let's be honest: We all have our own thoughts about marriage – what it is, when to do it, and the responsibilities therein.

These ideals are based on the examples and traditions we have been given. They have been tweaked and changed through experience, outcomes, and exposure to situations.

What this means is, when married, we may not agree with our spouse on everything.

What this does is make marriage hard.

Perhaps there is one thing on which we can agree: Marriage is a partnership, not a division of duties. It requires working together for the good of the union.

Somewhere in there should be balance. One person should not be doing everything. If that arrangement works for you and yours, great! But make regular assessments to verify both parties are happy. Chances are, if responsibilities are lopsided, there will be burn-out and brooding discontent. Remember the word is "helpmeet," not "help-slave." You are to come together, with each party contributing something.

The key is communication; this ability to work through "irreconcilable differences." My favorite definition: "Love is communication at its best." This applies physically, emotionally, mentally, and spiritually.

Intimacy is more than what happens in the bedroom. It is being able to discuss deepest fears, heartfelt desires, and darkest pain without backlash. It is allowing each person to expose vulnerability sans judgment.

Not an easy feat! No one wants to be put in a position where he might get hurt.

This is where marriage differs from dating. You don't get to leave after a couple of hours. Your other half is around all the time. Unless superhuman powers are thrown into the mix, you will experience a range of emotions as you interact under the same roof. Some of these moments will be more pleasant than others.

With routine, open conversations, however, you and your sweetheart can get back to the brass tacks and find what fits for you both.

Teach and Preach, Papa

It's a crazy world that keeps getting crazier, making the question spring eternal, "What will tomorrow bring?" and the answer, "Who knows?"

Regardless of what happens, we have multiple opportunities to make a difference – especially in the lives of our children, AKA the next generation.

It is a privilege to be entrusted with their care. It is a blessing to shower them with love. As parents (aunts, uncles, or Sunday school instructors), it is our opportunity to help children understand their importance, recognize their identity, and fulfill their potential.

A fundamental part of this responsibility is teaching them about comportment, such as good hygiene and manners. They don't come into the world knowing these things; these are learned. It takes practice to be able to sit still and listen. It takes work to master restraint; to wait to eat until everyone has sat down and to not run in the hallway.

And whereas it is okay to say yes, it is equally okay to say no. No to buying, eating, and collecting everything. No to doing this or that all the time. We do our children no favors by spoiling them, allowing them to think the whole ball of wax is and should be theirs. At some point, children must grasp this idea of sharing. They should learn how to handle disappointment, since life does not always go as expected. The effects of spoiling cannot be undone.

Likewise, it is more than acceptable to have your children act in certain ways. It is all right to send your children to bed at a decent hour or have them turn off certain programs. While yes, the ultimate goal is to have them reason for themselves, in the initial stages they don't have enough wisdom to make such decisions. It is our duty to lead.

Give them direction. It is not enough for them to wake up and breathe. Discuss values they can implement. Teach them how to be good citizens. Show them how to care.

Part of being a parent is parenting the child, not the other way around. Sometimes we think, "If I don't let him do this, he will be unhappy" or "She won't like me." They may even cry… for hours on end… in front of everyone we know!

Guess what? That, too, is okay. Children have feelings and moods the same as grown people. No one is happy all the time. What is important is to show them how to manage and manifest these sentiments in healthy ways. What is necessary is to find balance.

And of course, above all else, use love.

We Are Family

Scenario 1

- Have you heard from your grandbaby?
- Well, it took about four months, but she finally got back to me.
- And? Is it true?
- Yes, apparently, her post was the real deal.
- You're kidding.
- I wish I was.
- So, she actually got married?
- Mmm-hmmm.
- And she didn't invite you?
- She says she forgot.
- How do you forget a grandparent?
- I don't know. But she made sure she remembered her "bestie."
- Wow. Doesn't she love you at all?
- She *says* she does….

Scenario 2

- Is he coming?
- Not this year, babe. I'm sorry.
- I don't understand. Why not?
- Because he's going to the in-laws.
- Again? He's gone to the in-laws every year for every holiday for the last 17 years.
- I know.
- He sees them every other week.
- I know.
- What's the deal? Doesn't he love us?
- He *tells* me that he does…

Scenario 3

- Good news, dear.
- Yeah? What's that?
- I heard from your mom. She says she can't wait to visit.
- Yay! And what about your parents?
- They're good to go.
- Perfect. Then when it's time, I'll go by and pick up grandpa.
- I can do that for you. No problem.
- Great. Oh, and did you get that package mailed to your sister?
- I did.
- I just hate that she's going through a hard time. All that drama.
- Me too. But at least she knows we care.
- That's true. Hey, did I tell you my cousin and I are talking again?
- Why am I not surprised? You know you can never stay mad at him for long.
- I know, I know. Even though I don't always like what he does, we're still family.
- Yeah, and that's what it's all about.
- I know. Oh, and remember tomorrow's Tuesday. We'll be stopping by the nursing home to visit your uncle.
- That's right. Not to worry. I'll be ready.
- Okay. Well, then are you ready to eat?
- Absolutely. Here, let me get the door.
- Oh, honey. Have I told you lately how much I love you and our family?
- Well, no, not lately… but you sure have *shown* me.

Which would you rather?

Turn Around

Growing up my mom would always leave a to-do list for my brother and me to complete by the time she got home. None of the tasks were demanding; they just needed to get done. The bathtub required cleaning or the carpet vacuuming. It was a simple list, and if we put effort into it, we could finish it in under an hour. Then we were free to do whatever we pleased (so long as it was legal, of course).

As we got older, the list was no longer necessary. We could identify when the trash should be taken out or the dishes washed, and we simply did whatever it was. I guess you could say we evolved, becoming Vanilla Ice-ish in nature (as in "If there was a problem, yo I'll solve it!")

And that's how it should be, right? First, we receive instruction, and second, we adopt it into our lives, not waiting to be commanded in all things. At some point, we come to an understanding of what we can do to contribute and how it is not one person's responsibility to do everything. (How unfair it would be if it was!)

In families, we are teams, and when we work together, everyone wins. There is less stress and frustration, less dread of the mundane, higher productivity, and greater happiness. As a bonus, there is more time to do other desirable activities both individually and with one another.

And dum-dum-dum da da dum-dum... who wouldn't want that?

Player Wannabe

In high school, we had these sayings: "There is no 'I' in team" and "Together we can."

There was a real emphasis to focus on the whole rather than the one. If we could understand the value of teamwork, then we would realize higher success in everything from Class Wars to One-Acts. Correspondingly, application of this principle later in life would benefit company strategy, output, and sales revenue, amongst other things.

With combined effort, more energy is put toward the common good. This person pitches in here; this one shows up there. There is an increase in quality because all parties go the extra mile to fulfill their responsibilities to the best of their ability. Kobe doesn't do it all; it is a team victory.

The road to team playing, however, can be paved with unpredictable input. Lest we forget, everyone adds to the creative process in his or her own way, and that may or may not mesh with how you do things.

The trick is to amalgamate those ideas with yours (and everyone else's) for the benefit of the whole. Sometimes there will be compromise – a lot of it. At other times, you may have to scratch notions altogether and try an alternate approach.

In any case, do what you can for a genuine esprit de corps, because truly, the sum is greater than the parts.

THWARTING POWER-PLAY

By the power of Grayskull, I have the power... all the power... and you have none... or so I wish.

To have the ability to control, to ensure desired outcomes and truly get what you want – well, that seems to be something we all crave. It feels wonderful to be Charles in charge. What better way to win it all than with ultimate puissance?

But just like "more money, more problems," so too it is when it comes to power: The increase of influence can lead to unrighteous dominion. This, in turn, corrupts our ability to appreciate other viewpoints or make wise decisions in the interest of all.

As we study man's search for "God, gold, and glory," we learn that even the very best have succumbed to the impulse to pursue world domination, only to fall later. (Little wonder, there are too many people on the Earth for one person to overrule the rest.)

Hard as it may be, sometimes we have got to let go of the reins and let others share in leading. As we learn in elementary, "Together Everyone Achieves More" (TEAM). When we master the ability to consider ideas and delegate trust, we are bound to have favorable results. Our company will share genuine smiles, and our events will have better turnouts. We will boost respect one for another, enlarge morale, and learn to work together in an effective manner.

And *that* is what we call powerful.

Be Ye One

A favorite team-building exercise of mine goes as follows:

All participants stand close together in a circle facing the same direction. Each person places his hands on the shoulders of the individual standing in front of him. On the count of three, everyone sits down. If done correctly, each party seats comfortably on the lap of the person behind him in a balanced circle. (If not... well, you'll be a mess of giggles rolling around on the floor.)

Perhaps the symbolism is why I find it choice. The exercise epitomizes the principle of unity. It demonstrates how to interact with one another. It shows we can do so by:

1) Forming close relationships.
2) Sharing viewpoints.
3) Being inclusive.
4) Staying connected.
5) Doing our part.
6) Working toward the same goal.
7) Balancing weights and sizes (IE of problems).
8) Providing service and support.
9) Being comfortable with each other.
10) Moving together.

In the end, we are complete, like the circle. We are whole because we are united.

Said Lucy Mack Smith, "We must cherish one another, watch over one another, comfort one another and gain instruction that we may all sit down in heaven together" (*Relief Society Minutes*, Mar. 24, 1842, Archives of The Church of Jesus Christ of Latter-day Saints, 18-19).

Take a load off. Sit down together today.

The Heart of the Matter

As much as we hate to admit it, there are certain matters we cannot control, such as planetary movement or who wins the Oscar (unless it's La La Land).

Nor can we govern environment or an individual's choices; this is not The Truman Show, people have their agency.

And so, we must do as the Romans do, and adjust.

Crazy enough, while we have no authority over some issues, we do have power over ourselves. We can choose our actions, as well as our reactions, in various situations. We decide everything from what we wear to what we watch, from how we speak to where we go.

This includes what we ingest, be it fresh, steamed broccoli or yep-it's-gonna-give-me-acne-but-it'll-be-worth-it fried ice cream from the State Fair. Likewise, this idea encompasses media.

In that regard, please remember: Everything has a source.

To put it in black and white, thereby eliminating those 50 shades of gray, if a work is good, it will lead you to nobility; it will motivate you to be better. If a piece is subpar, so too then, is its aftermath.

Thus, it does matter what we consume visually and in print. For, as Raskolnikov would attest, thoughts do transfer into actions.

Let us choose, therefore, to partake of the wholesome oeuvres this world offers.

Cool it with the Force

There is almost nothing worse than someone trying to pressure you into doing something you don't want to do. "Go do this! Don't do that!" they repeat as they swarm menacingly around your ear.

And like any insect, you just want them to go away. Shoo please, and don't eat my blood. Leave me to rest in my hammock in peace.

It's crazy how some people are and how they think that's okay!

Of course, we would never act like that. No way would we ever force anyone to go along with something we want. If their heart wasn't into it, that would be it! We could let them be. We could dismiss all attempts to persuade them otherwise – first thing. Most assuredly, we wouldn't dare stoop to bribery... or stalking... or blackmail.

That wouldn't be fair... unless they're playing coy and want to maintain the argument.

Yeah. That must be it. They really want to do what we want, but they don't want us to know that they really want to do what we want. They want us to convince them. They want us to think we can "change their mind." Yeah. That's what it is. It has to be! But we know the truth.

Just in case, though, we should probably talk to them about it again...

Bzzzzzzzzzzzzzzzzzzzzz.

Smack.

There Will Always Be One

You think you have it. You're almost 100 % positive. How on earth could anyone say anything against it?

It is the perfect argument.

The one to silence the critics and shutdown the naysayers. It is articulate and supported by an overwhelming amount of data.

Then, it happens. Someone responds.

He criticizes every jot and tittle, and in one fell swoop, he seemingly demolishes the very case you had created. He, too, has facts – or alternative ones – that contradict your statement point-by-point! They aren't quite relevant to the topic at hand, which leaves you to wonder if he truly understood the pith of your concern. Based on his reply, he only heard what he wanted to hear.

There will always be one.

Rather than waste your precious strength preparing one retort after another, let it be.

What? And not get the last word? Clearly, he is wrong.

It doesn't matter.

Let it be.

But it's my responsibility – my civic duty – to show him what for, to set him straight.

Yeah, no, it isn't. Excepting life or death, listen to the Beatles, and let it be. You've said your peace. Leave it at that.

There are those who were born bellicose. It doesn't matter what you say; it doesn't matter how reasonable you are. The issue could be bagatelle. These people are going to bicker with the gate post until the bitter end. For every "comeforward," there will be a comeback.

As follows, there is no sense trying, because they are not ready to listen. Maybe one day that will change. Maybe it won't. He has his agency.

By stepping away, it doesn't make you wrong. By no means does it invalidate your thinking. Again, at this point, they aren't willing to receive; hence, if you belabor the issue, you'll only make yourself extremely tired.

Don't concern yourself with being right. Don't engage in the argument. Stay focused and free from such animosity by just walking away...

So Hung Up

For the love of all things decent... please don't answer the phone in the bathroom – especially a public one! Put it away before you come in. Wait the five or however long minutes it takes you to finish your business, and then return the call.

So what if you are BFFs to the moon and back! So what if you are comfortable with one another? No one wants to hear what you are doing. They need not be apprised of such "high" regard with a deafening flush. Plus, those around you don't want to share either, and they deserve their privacy.

Show some decorum.

Seriously, have we progressed so far that we can no longer see the line of decency? Where are the cookie crumbs?

Indeed, technology is a blessing. It has an excellent purpose. With today's phones, the cloud is the limit. There's even "K-blocker," should you wish to block all things Kardashian.

But these phones are going off and being answered everywhere! In addition to the potty-mouths, there are church clangors, funeral (dead)beats, and movie spoilers. Quality family-time is everyone phones-out for dinner. Forget that face-to-face conversation. How obsolete!

Put them on the road, and it's even worse. They cross into your lane multiple times without realizing it – at 7am and in a school zone! Talk about a wake-up call. Good thing laws are being passed.

Is it really that hard to remember to turn it off? Is it really that tough to break the addiction?

The answer is a ringing NO!

We are not pigs. We know how to curtail bad habits, and we are capable of self-discipline. There is a time and place for everything, and we know it. We are simply putting self-importance in the way.

It all boils down to respect... and maybe the reassurance that the world is not going to come to a harrowing end when you put your phone away. Your phone may "die" but certainly you won't (at least not today).

The Compliment Conspiracy? (Not hardly.)

With all that has happened as of late, we have lost a lot of trust in each other. In a world plagued with sarcasm and Internet trolls, that is to be expected.

And yet, I feel confident in also stating that there are still decent people in the world; those who mean exactly what they say. Several are in my family.

You may think otherwise, but life is not a conspiracy theory. The world is not out to get you or Mel. Get rid of this irrational paranoia of being judged; this crazed thinking that any statement anyone makes is a personal vendetta launched specifically against you, your family member, or someone in the community.

Sometimes a compliment is just a compliment, even if it is not given how you would like it to be. Believe it or not, compliments do not come with contingencies – or at least they shouldn't. There is no requirement that states, "If you say something about this, then you must say something about that too" or "If you don't mention this, then you are slighting that." That is simply ridiculous! And is it wrong to praise improvement? Absolutely not!

Should you continue to push for conditions, complimenting will stop altogether, leaving us in a world full of complaints.

We would do well to stop second-guessing, underestimating, and assigning ulterior motives to one another. That is what promotes contention.

If we are getting upset because someone's preferences differ from our own, then there is a greater, deep-seated problem at hand than we are willing to admit. Work on that before heaving false, hurtful attacks on someone else.

Moreover, we would be wise to spend time getting to know everyone on a profound level, thereby restoring trust and eliminating misunderstandings.

Considering Backlash

In reality TV, we take a lot of "journeys," and astonishingly, everyone is overly appreciative of the scripted progression.

In the news, we deal a lot with "backlash." This person "threw shade" at this other person when they "slammed" them with this "comment," Instagram, or recorded video. It goes viral within minutes. No one is safe – not even the recluse. And not a one of them seems happy about it.

It is such an interesting phenomenon. If anyone says anything that falls outside our echo chamber of beliefs, there is bound to be automatic backlash. Shame come to him. How dare he state something that does not mirror exactly what I think!?! Public floggings will be administered. Off with his head! Oh, and let's drag it out for days! Weeks! Years!

Even better, let's make fun. If anything, it'll help us get ahead. Who cares about feelings? Imitation, which used to be the highest form of flattery, is now the bully. We call it "shame culture."

You are dead set on the extreme, and then it happens to you... You become the subject of ridicule; the one everyone has turned against. Now it is you receiving the death threats and international shaming. You cannot leave your house. Forget about buying groceries.

Are you ready to handle the backlash? Are you prepared to deal with the emotional, mental, and other associated injuries?

Because it is not just going to go away. When it is no longer newsworthy, you will still have scars.

It sounds a bit extreme, doesn't it? And yet, it is in the news EVERY day and very rarely do we see the flipside: the receiver's pain. Let us ask ourselves: Are we adding to these social crucifixions? Are we resolving problems with our two cents or compounding them? What exactly is our contribution? How many will we find guilty in the court of public opinion without all the facts and a thorough investigation?

There is a difference between expressing opinion and being callous. There is line that separates teasing from harassment. And lest we forget, not everything is a social forum.

If we could all think before we speak, perhaps we could minimize – if not, eliminate – injuries, thus ensuring pleasant, unscripted journeys for everyone.

Having the Conversation

We speak a lot these days about "having the conversation." This theme is everywhere. In essence, it means – or at least what I take it to mean – is we, as members of society, need to have important discussions about difficult topics, be it politics, race, religion, gender, or anything else.

In many cases, people take to social media to express their thoughts, and that is fine. People should be allowed to state their beliefs.

This idea, though, that these social platforms equate to "holding conversations" is a bit stretched. Think about it. You go online; you post a comment. Apart from capitalization, punctuation, and maybe word choice, there is almost no tone. And if, by chance, there is some expression, it is limited. Your remark is only a summation of your sentiments, not a profound exploration. Somewhere along the way we reduced feelings to hashtags.

Then there is the turn around. You have sent your message into the great abyss called Cyberland, hoping to make some sort of connection. Some people will respond immediately, if they happen to be there; however, more often than not, there is going to be delay. People have to scroll through lengthy newsfeeds to get to what you are saying before they can read and reply. If they have thousands of friends, this could take a while. They may not even see it. There is no guaranteed reception. If they do, but happen to be in a hurry or aren't feeling up to it, you might just get a "like," "love" or crazy emoji – not actual dialogue. Some won't say anything. Others might, but given the restrictive speech, they could misunderstand you completely.

The point is, social media is superficial communication. It is not the way to "have the conversation." Conversation is oral; it is a dialogue. It is two or more people speaking audibly to one another (either in person or by phone or Skype), being able to exchange thoughts, ideas, and information immediately back and forth. When we do this, we effectively enable ourselves to understand one another and these deep-seated issues that are currently within our community.

SHHHHHH....

Let's get away. Fly away. Into the horizon. Whatcha think?

(Insert "Yeah, yeah, yeah" Lenny Kravitz-style.)

Sometimes life is just plain noisy. No matter where you go or what you do, a cacophony of tweets, bleeps, and "Chicken Fried" ringtones compete for your attention. It is a continual stream of audiovisual stimulation with advertisements and hip hop beats.

Given such non-stop distraction, it is a wonder we are still sane.

Not that I mind the modern world. I love the present day's "gadgets and gizmos a plenty." There are, however, moments I appreciate the beauty of silence.

There are times I must unplug.

It is about creating *Walden* on a personal, daily basis; a quiet time of introspection, self-renewal, enlightenment. The steady train of thought is put into park to appreciate the sweet scents of the mimosa tree.

Though it may seem like nothing, it is in these hushed instances where we can feel empowered. We are given peace-for-peace.

Blessed with inner serenity, the outside world no longer seems that loud.

Don't Shoot the Monster

In Mary Shelley's famous classic *Frankenstein*, a young doctor creates an eight-foot tall mutant with scientific genius and non-living matter. When finished, the result is far different than what he imagined: Instead of a beautiful creature, "the Adam of [his] labors" is ugly; therefore, Victor Frankenstein renounces him, referring to him as a "fiend" and "vile insect" (among other names).

Often through our actions, we, too, create monsters. When they are no longer picturesque, we reject them.

We forget that to every action, there is a consequence. Some are wonderful, and some are – shall we say – less than favorable. In many instances, the outcome may have been caused by something we said. Perhaps it was due to what was unsaid, since actions tend to speak louder than words. Whatever it was, be it our leadership, attitude, or trust (or the lack thereof), the product was of our own making.

We think, "Why is this person acting this way?" or "What is their problem?" failing to consider our part in the issue. We claim no responsibility, with a sort of "Billie Jean is not my lover" mentality. Sadly, we discount the other person's feelings, and the situation is exacerbated. (If you've read *Frankenstein*, then you know how dreadful the aftermath.) In some cases, we make ourselves the victim, the "broken" one.

If it was of a case of "we didn't know," now is certainly the time to respond with sensitivity.

And while, yes, people can and should control how they react to a problem, minimizing feelings does nothing to make the beast of an obstacle go away.

At some point, we must accept the dilemma and do what we can to make amends. We must own "the work of [our] hands," not destroy it.

Owning the Bad Guy Within

Have you ever noticed when people tell a story, more often than not, they play the victim? Or, in the rare instances they do admit to having erred, there is some sort of rationale to evoke pity?

In retrospect, are you finding you have been the same?

It is difficult owning the bad guy within. Intrinsically we want to be good, and we want people to like us. We would hate for others, especially our loved ones, to judge or turn away because of a mishap. We would feel horrible if we could not be forgiven. Truth be told, no one wants to be alone. And so, we manufacture excuse for our actions and generate justification for our words.

And yet, inevitably, with the nature of our species, we will make mistakes. There are occasions we could have harnessed our tongue or softened our approach. We could have redirected our intentions.

Basically, there will be many moments when we are wrong, like when we gossiped or failed to appear when needed. No one can escape imperfection. We might as well acknowledge this now.

The question is, "How do we handle it?"

Throughout my life, whenever I have related any type of tale, my mother has requested, in a soprano Jack Webb-ian sort of voice, "Just the facts, ma'am." I relay the information, and she makes a careful assessment of what transpired. I'll be honest – there have been times my mom has agreed with me, and there have been some in which she has not.

In cases where I misbehaved, my mother has instructed I –

1) Admit I was wrong,
2) Apologize, and
3) Make restitution.

Thanks to her correction, I have come to understand that if something Belittles And Demeans, then it is BAD. (This also applies to online behavior. It is inappropriate to be hateful just because there is anonymity).

When we take responsibility for the good and bad parts of ourselves, we improve our character. We progress in every way possible: spiritually, emotionally, socially. Others learn from what we share.

And hey, we have more interesting stories.

SUE HAPPY

These past few years there has been story after story about someone suing someone over something uber trivial, such as too much ice in the ice coffee, not enough length on the foot-long, or boredom at work. Remember the flying dinner roll?

The demands are incredible: Replace this $500 phone with $100,000. Give me a million (or more) dollars, a public apology, and share in your company. Fix my house. Upgrade my car. Send proceeds to my horse. The list goes on and on.

Ever since that preposterous McDonald's coffee incident, we have entered a world of frivolous lawsuits. Now, if something goes awry, our first thoughts are, "Don't worry, Sue Happy. No matter the matter, whether it is big or small, be captious and take it to court. Demand an exorbitant amount of everything, so all will be well, and you can have the life you always imagined. You deserve it. Your great-great-great grandchildren deserve it. This is the road to luxury. Then, and only then, will all be rectified."

Puh-lease!

First of all, these petty lawsuits are nothing short of robbery. They take money someone else has worked hard to earn, and give it to another. And for what? An accident? Human error? A small oversight? Sure, in some cases it may be justified (like with serious injury or illegal recordings) but for the most part, the demanded compensatory and punitive damages far exceed the actual distress caused by the Winnebago crash. Just because someone has a lot of money does not mean it is right to ask for a large piece of it. It is not yours. I don't care what the commercials say.

Second, joy does not come from being made rich instantly. (Check out the studies done on lottery winners.) We would all like to be financially stable, but there is a magic to earning money for yourself that can never be replaced by a court's legal recompense. Where there is sweat, there is appreciation.

Third, in most of these instances, what is needed is common sense and forgiveness. If you don't like a product, don't buy it. If you are dissatisfied with a service, go somewhere else. Wear sunglasses. Don't drive by. No need to ruin it with your caviling. Not everyone feels the same way you do.

If you are unhappy with someone, have a heart-to-heart. If that doesn't redress the problem, make new friends. Talk to other people. There are alternative ways to resolve disputes that still 'prove a point' but stay out of the courtrooms, which are overloaded as it is. Certainly, we can find healthy ways to deal with our anger over perceived injustices.

Suing should be the exception, not the rule. When in doubt, repeat that to yourself. Again. Suing is the exception, not the rule.

FORGIVENESS AND ALL THAT STUFF

Here it is: Real time, real talk.

There is an awful lot of wrongdoing happening in the world. Oftentimes it feels like you are getting the short end of the stick, while everyone else skyrockets to the top – even 'sworn enemies.'

It's hard. It's annoying. It's frustrating beyond belief.

Someone 'does you wrong' – and boom! – there they go! Success galore.

And here you are, trying with everything not to hate them forever. How on earth do you get past it?

Well, honestly, you may not. It might be one of those things that impacts your life forever. You may not be able to forget, and that's okay. The friendship could be ruined; the trust demolished. You'll have to find a new bestie to sing late-night karaoke with you.

The essential part of forgiveness is being able to rise above the negative feelings you have toward someone. You know, the ones that make you want to run him over with your car and take up voodoo. A plague on both your houses...and lawnmowers. May you never find your tweezers again!

These feelings are toxic, and the longer you hold onto them, the more they will destroy you – not the other person. They will canker your spirit and imprison your soul. You won't be able to think about anything else; hatred will become your obsession. In such a state, there can be no progression, for you are bound.

Letting go is a process. It is not easy to look past offenses and ascend above acrimony. For most, it will require a ton of prayer to procure heaven's help to be civil. (You might want to throw in a few Yoga classes as well.)

BUT... it can be done. If you are determined, it is possible.

And the freedom you feel as you purge the rancor – well, it is almost as if you are flying.

Breaking the Seal

There is a feeling that, most likely, all of us will experience at one time or another; a hard-to-shake sentiment that pulls at our very heartstrings, urging us to abandon hope and surrender to a harsh reality.

It is called despair, and it brings out that infamous "ugly cry." Maybe even a million of them, since it leads us to believe that the windows and doors of opportunity are forever sealed against us. It's this idea that "Everyone else gets the dream. Everyone else… that is, everyone else but me."

It would be so simple to give up, settle, and live on milkshakes for the rest of your life. What's the point, right? The heavens have been impenetrable. Who isn't sick of buying tissue for all these breakdowns?

But we are made of sterner stuff (as are our ambitions). We are tougher than we realize, and sometimes we need time to prove that to ourselves.

Somehow, we have to find the strength to chisel our way forward and tap into that feeble-yet-persistent little something that whispers, "Keep trying. Don't give up. Your tears will turn into joy – and soon."

There is a heavenly balm that can touch our hearts and make things better, especially when others have let us down and life is going nowhere.

Although we cannot see the how or when, whatever-it-is will happen, and there will be sweet release.

Arms Folded, Fingers Crossed

It's hard to believe in the unseen; to go beyond the realm of realistic into the world of impossible, believing miracles can happen.

For even if they did, wouldn't that be improbable, like turning plain yellow pumpkins into golden carriages?

But what if missions were possible and the inconceivable conceivable? (Or the incovfefe covfefable?) Is that really difficult to accept? Would that be so preposterous? Somehow James Bond manages to stay alive...

Unexplained phenomena happen every day, and try as we may, we can't always pinpoint what is going on. Our minds are limited in understanding; our wisdom is meager. Though we would like to think otherwise, we don't know it all, nor can we process everything. Even at Sears Tower, we might get an overall picture but miss many of the details.

At some point, we have to believe our dreams will come true, and we have to pray like we want them (AKA with real intent). It might be the biggest challenge we've ever taken, to extend beyond our thinking borders, but somewhere in there we must learn to trust God.

We cannot discount His capabilities or the way He loves us. He wants us to have the best, which means He will make things happen. He will provide the manna.

When all else seems impractical, remember: Hope coupled with prayer equals the realization of personal marvels.

Determination Decision

I'm not sure about you, but sometimes I engage in these sort of thoughts (particularly when I am feeling tired and low):

"Why can't I have that? Why don't I have that? I've done far more than those people... I'm better than them. Really? They're allowed to procreate? After they did THAT? Nooooo! Stop the madness now."

Obviously, these aren't what we would call "the most uplifting thoughts."

But they come every now and again by way of temptation. It feels normal to tally up our "rights" against another person's "wrongs" to justify why we deserve something more than him or her.

And yet, who are we to make that determination? We are not omniscient. There's no way we know better than He what is best for ourselves and others.

When we make these judgments, we underestimate His power and His timing. We are misplacing confidence, directing it into our wisdom rather than His.

Even if nothing makes sense, one of these days, we are going to have to believe He knows what He is doing. This is no picnic. A nun could get frustrated. We may have to repeat truth, promises, and past miracles to ourselves daily to maintain conviction and bonhomie. We may want to get introspective. Most definitely, we will need to train ourselves to cast off negative thoughts as soon as they come upon us.

Also, it is important to learn how to be happy for others, regardless of what is or what is not happening in our lives. Life is not a comparison of newsfeeds.

Additionally, people are always going to make mistakes. It is not our place to dictate whether those faults should impact their reception and number of blessings.

Decide now to let Him make that determination, and find peace of mind.

The Heartful Referee

Sometimes in this crazy game we call life, doors aren't just closed, they weren't options in the first place. There are zero opportunities. Time passes and because life doesn't parallel such-and-such who seems to have it sooooooooooooo easy, we feel stuck in this terrible, never-ending inning. Or, we think that we have been permanently ousted, having struck out earlier on the play. For this reason, we'll never win. Tattoo an FL on the forehead; we are Forever Losers.

In these moments, when we feel utterly beaten, we are prone to blame God. After all, if He really is over all, then why doesn't He arbitrate the game better? He lets the other guy hit, and He lets him score! These people have earned run after run, sometimes cheating on the play, while we have gotten nothing. Is He just rigging it for our failure? Does He want us to fail?

Lest we forget, God has said, "My thoughts are not your thoughts" (Isaiah 55:8).

Our minds are finite. We see things one – maybe two or three – ways. It is hard for us to comprehend alternatives, especially any that stray from the path we had envisioned. Moreover, in the midst of them, we fail to grasp how they could possibly be superior to what we would have picked for ourselves. We think "decent little cottage," whereas God wants "palace" (C. S. Lewis).

Then we hear it... People saying again and again, "God is preparing you for something else" or "Something bigger must be coming. Just be patient." We are quick to dismiss this optimism because we've lost heart. Doesn't He know we are ready? Why does it still feel stagnant?

We must remember two points: One, everything is a process, and two, our lives are unique.

Nothing happens overnight. We witness this everywhere, from construction of roads to preparing a meal to growing vegetables to sewing an outfit to cleaning to learning an instrument to developing a skill to saving millions of dollars and so on. Us wee mortals don't have Jeannie's advantage; we must work continually for what we want, no matter how long it takes, and believe me, it takes time.

Hindsight makes it easier to recognize the Lord's hand. For peace of mind, pray for the ability to see what He is doing today.

In addition, our lives don't flow the same direction as anyone else. We might have similar experiences (because we're in the same game), but they aren't identical. There are always variables. God has created us as individuals, not clones; therefore, our journey is particular to us. This person may have achieved what we wanted at 22, and that's wonderful. We are not that person, and isn't that something? We're not a carbon-copy; God has given us more thought. There's an element of surprise for these adventures that await us.

Don't let yourself get fixated on what you feel you are missing. In any game, there are several elements at play – many of them unseen. Trust in the justice and mercy of God. As you learn more about Him, you will discover that He has your best interest at heart. Know that as you keep swinging, He will reconcile you to victory.

READY, SET, FIGHT

Recently, I met a person who was facing a difficult and rather unusual situation. After sharing details, he concluded with the questions, "Well, wouldn't you give up? Wouldn't you stop caring?"

To his surprise, my answer to both was an adamant, "No. Don't fight your battles with apathy."

If the blessing is worth having, then most assuredly, it merits the fight. Maybe not the step-into-the-ring-throw-down-against-Danny-Garcia-fisticuff type of affair, but certainly, the crusade requires the same amount of effort. To guarantee success, to witness the miracle, we must stay engaged with what we can do, not waiting for Fairy Godmother to appear.

Yes, there are moments we must exercise restraint; there are occasions to repress sentiment. Some situations require Tolstoy's "powerful warriors" of "patience and time." This does not mean we cease to feel. We are not statues. We were created to love and care for people and causes.

And of course, remember to ask of God, not of Google. He's in your corner, ready to come in.

So, strap on the gloves and prepare for combat – we're here past the long count.

Success Unlimited

Sometimes you can't help but think, "Man, that guy has everything!"

Some people just walk in the light, you know?

They have the ideal: an awesome job, a sweet car, money galore, a prominent position, recognition and status, a great marriage, obedient children, a fabulous house, good genetics, a killer fashion sense, inventions, awards and honors, a striking resemblance to this year's hottest celebrity, and season tickets to the Knicks.

And well, you... you feel this desperate need to hide in the shade. In juxtaposition, you are puppy chow. Or the pus that infects the mucus that cruds up the fungus... Sorry. Great movie.

But let's get real, shall we?

Life is not about eyeing the neighbor's grass, panting after the Joneses, or keeping up with the Kardashians. Forget about them. Our achievements are not determined by comparisons to other people. If anything, we are in a race against past versions of ourselves; in a quest to shake bad habits and to become better than what we once were.

Please note you don't have to be at the top of everything to have success – to experience even a modicum of success. Victory comes in what may be considered small or unnoticeable moments, and achievement is attainable on multiple levels. At its core, it is about making a positive difference.

Keep going! Keep on dreaming!

Extend the parameters of success to include those "little" things.

Ralph Waldo Emerson defined it best:

What is success?
To laugh often and much;
To win the respect of intelligent people
And the affection of children;
To earn the appreciation of honest critics
And endure the betrayal of false friends;
To appreciate beauty;
To find the best in others;
To leave the world a bit better, whether by
A healthy child, a garden patch
Or a redeemed social condition;
To know even one life has breathed
Easier because you have lived;
This is to have succeeded.

With that, you are a victor who walks in the sunshine.

While you're at it, make sure to walk through some sprinklers, too!

www.ingramcontent.com/pod-product-compliance
Lightning Source LLC
Chambersburg PA
CBHW061429040426

42450CB00007B/971